D0252972

# REMEMBER EVERYTHING
## YOU READ

# REMEMBER EVERYTHING YOU READ

## The Evelyn Wood Seven-Day Speed Reading and Learning Program

Dr. Stanley D. Frank

TIMES T BOOKS

RANDOM HOUSE

Copyright © 1990 by American Learning Corporation

All rights reserved under International and Pan-American Copyright Conventions. Published in the United States by Times Books, a division of Random House, Inc., New York, and simultaneously in Canada by Random House of Canada Limited, Toronto.

Library of Congress Cataloging-in-Publication Data
Frank, Stanley D.
   Remember everything you read: the Evelyn Wood seven-day speed reading and learning program/Stanley D. Frank.
      p.   cm.
   ISBN 0-8129-1773-1
   1. Study, Method of.   2. Rapid reading.   I. Title.
LB1049.F65   1990
371.3′028′2—dc20                                            89-20494

Manufactured in the United States of America

# ACKNOWLEDGMENTS

I'm especially grateful to the following people:

Evelyn Wood, who pushed through the knowledge frontier and in the process helped millions of people recognize their own achievement potential.

Dan Warner, for his personal commitment to the Evelyn Wood method over the past two decades, and for his contributions to the many vignettes throughout the book.

William Proctor, who has spent countless hours assisting the author with field interviews and manuscript development.

# Contents

Introduction      ix

**1.** Mental Soaring: The Secret to Success      3

**2.** The First Step Toward Mental Soaring:
"Subsonic" Reading      19

**3.** Mapping Out Your Academic Flight Plan      42

**4.** The Takeoff for Rocket-Powered
Reading and Learning      67

**5.** How to Fly with Your Hands      88

**6.** Preparing Your Own "Mental
Computer Printout"      109

**7.** The Secret of Merging with Your
Instructor's Mind      129

**8.** Supersonic Writing      140

**9.** How Fast Can You Go?      158

**10.** The Thrill of the Final Test Flight:
Using Your New Skills to Ace the Exam      175

**11.** Shooting For the Stars      199

Index      203

# *Introduction*

Ordinary reading skills won't do in today's world because there is too much information and too little time to assimilate it. If you read at the average speed of 250 words per minute, you're at a major disadvantage trying to take in the facts and concepts you need to perform well in school or on the job. For that matter, you're at a severe disadvantage even at speeds of 400–600 words per minute—a rate that's in the top range for the most experienced students and adults.

So what is the solution to this dilemma?

After years of experience as an educator and publishing executive, I've become convinced that the techniques we've developed at Evelyn Wood are by far the best response to the information explosion. Furthermore, our approach provides the fastest, most effective path to superior academic achievement.

For the first time in a book for the general public, I'm unveiling all the secrets that have made the completely revised Evelyn Wood dynamic learning program so effective and popular. As a result of this candor, we hope to introduce millions of additional people to the exciting possibilities of Mental Soaring, as I call the dynamic learning experience.

Our goal for the nation's students is bold, to say the least: We want record numbers to achieve "supersonic" reading skills and honors-level academic performance. Yet I'm convinced that this goal can be realized if you practice the principles set forth in these pages.

High school and college students and their parents will initially evince the most interest in this book. On the other hand, even fifth-graders have been very successful in employing our reading and learning techniques.

As for adults, men and women of all ages and in every occupation can benefit, especially from the discussions on speed reading, improving comprehension and scientific note-taking. And of course, there are millions of adults who have taken the original Evelyn Wood courses over the years and who may want to brush up on old skills or perhaps learn new ones.

Now, as you prepare for the exciting adventure of Mental Soaring, I want to encourage you to leave behind all your preconceptions about reading, learning, studying and academic achievement. There are no ceilings to what you can accomplish so long as you're ready and willing to let the natural power of your mind move you toward a new realm of intellectual reality.

Stanley D. Frank, Ed.D.

# REMEMBER EVERYTHING
## YOU READ

# 1

# *Mental Soaring: The Secret to Success*

What does it take to be a superior student?

The most important secret to being a contender for the top of the class has always been effective reading—and that means reading that involves:

1. high-speed assimilation and comprehension of all sorts of subject matter; and
2. the ability to recall that subject matter later during testing.

The superior student, then, is one who first of all can read assigned books and handouts quickly and understand thoroughly what has been read. Second, he is able to collect the material he's read into well-organized personal notes and then draw on his memory of these notes when confronted with examination questions.

In addition to having outstanding reading abilities, the topflight student knows how to listen in class—knows how to absorb key concepts during oral presentations and how to take notes on lectures. Finally, he can recall what he has heard and use it effectively at test time.

In some ways, all this may sound quite simple. But let's be honest: We know that only a few students really know how to make this formula work. Yet when understood and applied, these skills are the foundation for what I call Mental Soaring—a phenomenon that goes so far beyond traditional studying that the best student seems to be flying through academic material at the highest levels of comprehension.

These are the basic skills—the secrets, if you will—that have been mastered by the elite students who get into the best schools. Furthermore, they are the skills typically used by the small percentage who perform with flying colors after they've been admitted to various colleges and universities.

So where does this leave the not-so-stellar student? Is it inevitable that these special skills and secrets must remain in the academic arsenal of only a small coterie of geniuses or near-geniuses?

Absolutely not! These techniques can enhance the learning potential of *any* student. The only problem up to now has been that no one has bothered to tell the average or mediocre student what the top academic performers already know: that good students aren't born—they're made.

To correct the misconception that academic ability is inborn, those of us in charge of the reading and learning programs at Evelyn Wood and the Britannica Learning Centers have decided that the time has arrived to reveal these fundamental secrets to academic success. Using the methods described in this book, many students have tripled their reading speeds and increased their comprehension in our Center programs.

## *A First for the General Public*

For the first time in any book or publication for the general public, I'm presenting all of the essential techniques involved in the Evelyn Wood reading and learning system. This information is designed to be used by anyone with at least fourth-grade reading skills.

Among other things, you will learn:

- How to raise reading speed by at least 50 percent in less than an hour of study and practice, using certain key techniques.
- How to at least double reading speed, with increased comprehension, after one week.
- How to reach the stratosphere of speed reading—the 1,200–3,000-word-per-minute range—and perhaps go beyond.
- How to improve concentration and attention span.
- How to enhance analytical abilities, overall learning capacity, and memory.
- Practical programs to raise performance levels—and grades—in all subjects, including the humanities, social sciences, physical sciences and mathematics.
- Techniques to improve test-taking abilities.
- Proven approaches for taking the most effective notes during lectures; and
- Tips and strategies for increasing efficiency and achieving success in doing research and writing term papers.

## *What Does This Mean for You?*

Now, let's take this discussion down to the most practical level: How can you acquire these all-important abilities?

I've said that these important skills can be learned; they aren't simply inherent intellectual capacities that good students are born with. Let me illustrate by getting you involved at the outset in a hands-on exercise that will prove it's possible to improve your reading speed dramatically and almost instantaneously.

———

This exercise is designed to identify your present reading speed—an important piece of information if you hope to learn how to improve your reading and study rates. After you've completed the exercise, you may want to let your youngster try it in order to determine his or her speed.

Here's how it works: Using a watch with a second hand, note the precise minute and second now shown on your watch. (You need to record this time on a piece of paper *right now* so that you don't forget.)

Next, begin reading the remainder of this chapter now at your normal rate. BEGIN READING NOW.

Keep your watch, pencil and pad close at hand, and continue reading until the direction to stop later in this text.

———

At Britannica Learning Centers—where the Evelyn Wood reading and study concepts have become a staple of our student preparation programs—we know that almost anyone can learn the study techniques employed by superior students. These skills are not based on difficult or arcane principles reserved for the elite or supersuccessful. Rather, they can be learned by practically any individual, regardless of educational background or prior level of achievement— so long as that person is willing to make a relatively modest commitment of time and effort.

Before you've finished this opening chapter, you'll be given some simple tools designed to increase your present reading speed by at least 50 percent immediately. In another seven days, you can expect a quantum leap forward to much higher reading and comprehension levels. And finally, with a reasonable amount of practice in subsequent weeks, you'll find that the sky is indeed the limit for enhancing your learning speed and capacity.

Of course, many of the elite and supersuccessful have already been impressed by the Wood approach. The Evelyn Wood Reading Dynamics Program, which began in 1959, has been promoted and praised by three U.S. presidents:

- John F. Kennedy, himself a very fast reader, brought teachers from Evelyn Wood into the White House to help increase the speed of top-level members of his staff.
- Richard Nixon commended the Wood program for teaching members of his staff.
- Jimmy Carter actually took the course himself—and reportedly achieved a 1,200-word-per-minute reading rate, with high comprehension.

On the grassroots level, during its thirty-year history, the Wood program has helped more than two million people read faster, more efficiently, and with improved comprehension and retention. The other learning and studying skills that have been added to the speed-reading program over the years—such as high-powered note-taking and successful test-taking—have greatly enhanced the average student's chances of improved grade-point averages.

# Why Superior Reading and Study Skills Are So Important

Most American students, even those with the greatest native intelligence, perform well below their potential in school. Moreover, their below-par showing continues after they graduate and enter the working world. Too many do poorly in writing, reading and other occupational tasks that require significant intellectual abilities.

In fact, more than 95 percent of college-bound high school seniors lack the necessary reading skills to enable them to succeed in their college, business, and professional lives, according to a recent U.S. Department of Education study. Also, 50 percent of students who enter college never graduate.

Why do so many students have so many academic problems?

Obviously, there are numerous complex socioeconomic factors that play a role in our students' poor performance. But not every such factor demands profound societal or political action to produce beneficial change.

One major cause of our problems is that our students have been conditioned to expect that they must read and study at a slow, boring speed. Yet moving along at a snail's pace isn't at all necessary, and it's almost always counterproductive.

In fact, to maintain a high level of interest and efficiency in study, it's absolutely essential to assimilate information faster. Otherwise, boredom and lower levels of academic performance are almost inevitable.

Let's see why this is so.

The average person (and that includes the average student) reads at a rate of about 250 words per minute. Yet that same "average" person has been estimated to think at an astounding rate of more than 50,000 words per minute!

If this is true—and certainly we all know that we think much, much faster than we read—is it any wonder that many students get frustrated and bored when they read? Their lightning-fast minds are ready to take in incredible amounts of information. But their painfully slow reading thwarts them and leads to mind-wandering.

On a number of occasions, I've heard highly accomplished friends and colleagues complain along these lines:

"If only I could read and absorb information as quickly as I can think. But that's impossible. If I could do that, I'd be superhuman!"

Perhaps this idea of learning at extremely high speeds isn't quite so farfetched or fanciful as you might think. Granted, it may not be possible to read or learn at 50,000-plus words per minute. But how about 3,000?

## *How Richard Learned to Soar*

Consider what happened to Richard, a high school senior who took one of our three-week Evelyn Wood reading courses.

He had been progressing quite well and had increased his reading speed from just under 300 words per minute to just over 1,000, according to the most recent test he had been given.

Many of our students end up reading faster than this, however, and Richard's fast-developing skills suggested that he might increase his speed significantly if he kept practicing. His instructor expected him to be pushing 1,200 to 1,500 words per minute before he completed his work.

Toward the end of the course, however, something odd happened. Along with the other students, Richard was assigned several short books to read in class, the last of which graphically detailed the nuclear bombing and devastation of Hiroshima at the end of World War II. The instructor later recalled that she had been timing the class for only a few minutes as they read the Hiroshima book when Richard turned his volume over and walked out of the room.

"My husband was waiting out in the hallway for the class to finish, and when he saw Richard come out, he thought the boy was sick," she said. Apparently, the young man had turned quite pale and seemed extremely nauseated.

At the next break, the instructor, who had been apprised of the situation by her husband, approached Richard and asked, "Are you all right?"

"Yes," he replied, "but something strange happened to me in there."

"What was that?"

"As I was reading, the words seemed to come off the page and become a motion picture. I saw—literally *saw*—the bombing and what happened to those Japanese people! And I got sick."

"You finished the entire thing?" the instructor asked, knowing that the book was more than a hundred pages long.

When the boy nodded, the teacher went over and checked the time he had spent reading the book. After a quick calculation, she discovered that Richard had been reading at more than 3,000 words per minute. Furthermore, a quiz on the book showed that he was reading with more than 90 percent comprehension.

Think for a moment about the implications of this experience: If the average student reads at 250 words per minute, it will take him nearly seven hours to read a two-hundred-page book (assuming that there are five hundred words to the page). But if that same student begins soaring along at the rate of 3,000 words per minute, he or she will be able to complete the same book in less than thirty-five minutes.

Is this really possible? It is indeed—for those who are willing to learn and apply the principles and guidelines I'll be describing. In fact, I can guarantee that with serious practice, most students and parents can move up to 1,000 words per minute in only a few weeks. And if you continue to work at fine-tuning these reading and learning skills, it's possible to move even faster—perhaps up to and beyond Richard's achievement.

In the following pages you'll be shown in detail many ways to increase your reading speed and enhance other learning skills. Specifically, you'll learn:

- How to calculate your reading speed.
- The famous—and fundamental—Evelyn Wood speed-reading hand motions, with illustrative diagrams.
- The "layering" technique of assimilating written material (also called the Multiple Reading Process), which is the essential foundation for high-speed reading.
- How to plan a study strategy, with suggestions for setting up monthly and weekly calendars.
- Time- and energy-saving techniques for using lectures and class discussions as a warm-up for study.
- The highly effective "recall pattern" concept for taking notes—including a detailed description of the famous "slash recall pattern" used effectively by many top students.

11

- How a student's ability to use important material on tests can be improved during the "postview" phase of reading.
- Specific methods for achieving success on both essay and short-answer exams.
- How to break through the "subsonic reading barrier" of 800–900 words per minute by applying the secret of "visual-vertical" reading.

In one St. Louis school district, which had been performing quite poorly on standard tests, only one-third of the eighth-grade students passed a Basic Essential Skills Test (BEST) in 1985. This test included questions on reading, language arts, math, government and economics. But the next year, after the students took a special Evelyn Wood course, 75 percent passed.

In the same school, a group of twenty sixth-graders increased their reading scores by an entire grade level after taking a five-week Evelyn Wood course. Their average reading speed jumped from 115 words per minute to 234 words per minute. Overall, 82 percent of the students increased their comprehension and vocabulary reading levels, and 94 percent increased their reading rates.

These and other similar results have convinced me that our reading and study program can transform the intellectual productivity of boys and girls, as well as that of men and women at almost every age level. We've encountered significant success with students from the fifth grade on up. But to emphasize just how the lives of young people of different ages can be changed dramatically, let me introduce you now to three students—a sixth-grader, an eighth-grader and a newly arrived college freshman.

# It's for Every Student, Regardless of Age

**Sandra, the sixth-grader.** An extremely conscientious girl, twelve-year-old Sandra found she was spending most of her evenings on schoolwork. She was always studying, preparing reports, and reading books assigned to her. Furthermore, she was losing far too much sleep as she tried to keep up with her workload. "We had little or no family time together," her mother recalled.

But then, Sandra learned and began to apply to her work the same principles you'll find in this book. Just a few weeks later, her life and the life of her family had completely changed. Instead of reading an average 250–300 words per minute, she had "taken off" and was soaring at more than 1,500 words per minute—with increased comprehension.

Sandra's mother reported shortly afterward, "We have more family time available now. Her schoolwork is completed in a relatively short period, and she also has time to spend on pleasure reading. And amazingly, Sandra now goes to bed at a reasonable hour!"

**Timothy, the eighth-grader.** Like many fourteen-year-olds, Timothy was sure he knew more about how to do his schoolwork than his parents did. So for weeks, he resisted trying the learning and reading methods that we advocate at our Britannica Learning Centers.

But there was another powerful factor operating with Timothy: peer pressure. He wanted to do well in school and in fact, he *had* been doing quite well. But he was also beginning to pay a price. Even though some of his classmates seemed to breeze through their work, he found he had to spend hours reading the required books and doing the other homework assignments.

13

It appeared that Tim might have to cut out some of his extra activities, such as one of his sports teams, in order to keep up with his studies. The whole experience was becoming so discouraging that he was getting frustrated and was losing his motivation to excel at school.

So finally Tim decided to go along with his parents' suggestion to try the Wood-Britannica approach, which was being offered at a center near his school. Like many others who had followed the same route, Tim immediately began to reap the benefits of faster reading and learning.

His most significant early payoff from the course came when he was given a major reading and writing assignment at his school. His class was told to read a book that was more than three hundred pages long and then to write an essay and prepare for a test on the book. Furthermore, this requirement was imposed in addition to his regular homework, and it had to be completed within two weeks.

Quite an assignment for many eighth-graders—but Tim came through in fine style. Using his new speed-reading and note-taking skills, he finished the book in only two evenings. As a result, he had plenty of time to work on the essay, which he completed at the end of the first week. After that, he faced a relatively relaxed few days studying for the test.

His grades? An A on the essay, and an A on the exam. Not only that, Tim had found that during those two weeks he still had plenty of time available for his extracurricular activities.

**Marsha, the college freshman.** After taking an Evelyn Wood course for only a couple of weeks, Marsha discovered that her reading speed had increased from about 350 words per minute to more than 1,300 words per minute, with excellent comprehension. Then, unexpectedly, she found herself in the challenging position of having to use her newly acquired knowledge at school.

"On Friday, I missed one of my classes," she said. "When I came in on Monday, I learned—to my shock—that we were going to have a test in one of my courses on fifty pages of material that I hadn't read. And the class was scheduled to begin in only twenty minutes!"

So what did Marsha do? She didn't panic. Instead, she turned a potential nightmare into a triumph. Since she knew her instructor was a tough case who didn't look kindly on excuses, she immediately realized that she had only three choices. She could skip the test and take a failing grade; or try to read as much as she could at her old 350-word-per-minute rate, and then fake it when questioned about the material she hadn't reached; or attempt to use her newly acquired high-speed reading techniques.

Fortunately, Marsha chose the third option. "I figured this was going to prove to me whether or not the method really works," she said. "And it *did* work in this case. I got through all the material in the allotted twenty minutes; I understood it all; and I aced the test."

Clearly, the possibilities of reading and learning faster and more efficiently are enormous. But how exactly can you—or the student in your home—achieve these results?

That's what the rest of this book is about: exploring and explaining how anyone can learn the art of mental soaring. Learning these high-powered reading and studying techniques is somewhat analogous to flying an airplane. At the outset, you have to become familiar with the controls on your plane, the fundamentals of flight, and a variety of other basic aeronautic facts and principles. Then, you're ready to take off and try your wings.

But in flying a necessary preliminary step is to have a

flight physical to establish the precise current status of your mental and physical faculties. It's similar with Mental Soaring. You need to evaluate your reading ability at the beginning so that you'll have a baseline to let you know how much and how quickly you're improving.

You'll recall that I asked you to begin timing your reading several pages back. Well, now is the time to STOP.

Look at your watch and record the precise minute and second.

———

Now you can calculate your reading speed by following these three steps:

**Step 1:** Figure how many minutes and seconds have passed since you first began to keep track of the time for this exercise.

Suppose, for example, that your watch indicated 10 seconds past 9:16 P.M. when you started, and it's now 30 seconds past 9:27 P.M. In that case, you've been reading precisely 11 minutes and 20 seconds.

**Step 2:** Convert the number of minutes and seconds that you read into a decimal figure.

To do this, just divide by 60 (the total number of seconds in one minute) the number of extra seconds you recorded in excess of the whole-minute figure. Then insert the number of whole minutes before the decimal point, and you've got your decimal number.

In our example, you'd divide the 20 extra seconds you recorded by the 60 seconds in a whole minute, and this would give you .33. Then, before the decimal point, you insert the 11 whole minutes you recorded, and that will give you 11.33 minutes that were spent reading.

16

**Step 3:** Divide the number of minutes you read (as calculated in Step 2) into 2,700. This figure, 2,700, is the approximate number of words that you read between the instruction BEGIN READING NOW on page 6 and the instruction STOP on page 16. This calculation will provide you with the number of words per minute at which you have been reading so far in this book.

Now to apply this step to our illustration, divide 11.33 into 2,700, and you'll end up with just over 238 words per minute—a rate close to the average 250-words-per-minute reading speed of most people, including most junior high and high school students.

If you read faster than 250, that's great. Or if you read at a slower rate, that's fine too. In any case, *whatever* your speed is now, you can expect to increase it by at least 50 percent almost immediately.

To accomplish this, all you have to do is apply these simple techniques, which I'll describe in greater detail in the next chapter of this book:

• Be sure that you're now reading in a comfortable environment.

   You should be using or have at hand such essentials as a comfortable chair, a solid desk or writing surface, good lighting, and a quiet room. Unless the atmosphere is reasonably conducive to effective reading, your ability to concentrate and immerse yourself thoroughly and enjoyably in the subject matter will be impaired.

• As you read, pace yourself by moving a finger across the page, line by line.

   Start from left to right on this line of print, and then return your hand like a typewriter carriage to the left-hand margin, so that it can move again from left to right on the next line below. Move your pacing hand along at a comfortable speed, but don't feel you have to rush. Your eyes should trail along just behind your pacing finger.

- Don't regress as you read.

   That is, don't allow yourself to stop at any point and look back over what you've already read. Instead, force yourself to move ahead, even if you think you've missed something or your attention has temporarily wandered.

- Try to take in groups of words as you read, rather than looking at each word individually.

   But do this in a comfortable way. In other words, if you feel relaxed taking in only two or three words at a time, don't feel compelled to try for four or five words.

If you're a parent, share some of these very simple, fundamental principles with your child, and encourage him to try them as often as possible. Chances are, he'll experiment for a while and then threaten to give up because "it's too hard" or "it doesn't feel right." But expect such a reaction because that's the kind of initial response that may be triggered by the learning of any new skill.

In any event, don't push him. Just suggest a few of these techniques and continue to work on them yourself. Your pleasure, as your own reading speed and enthusiasm increase, will be the best argument to convince your child.

By the time you reach the end of this book—and learn and practice other skills I'll show you—your learning capacity should increase dramatically and your original reading speed should double, triple, quadruple, or soar to even higher rates.

# 2

# The First Step Toward Mental Soaring: "Subsonic" Reading

Mental Soaring—the term I use for the high-speed, super-efficient assimilation and organization of printed materials —involves a wide array of skills that students must develop gradually, over a period of weeks and months.

Still, there are some simple, easy-to-master techniques that can increase anyone's reading speed by 50 percent or more overnight. These fundamental principles can, by themselves, revolutionize studying immediately.

Furthermore, these basic techniques are a necessary first step for the student who wants to reach the upper ranges of fast reading and effective learning. In other words, he who hopes eventually to soar must first move systematically, step by step, from one skill plateau to the next. Only in this way can the student hope to build a repertoire of skills that will eventually emerge in "supersonic" learning ability.

The first step in Mental Soaring, then, is to understand what might be called the skill of "subsonic" academic flight. But what exactly does this involve? To begin with, it's important to understand a few things about what might be called your hidden voice.

## Your "Hidden Voice"

Everyone's reading—except for those expert in the special Evelyn Wood learning skills—involves two dominant characteristics:

1. The reading is accompanied by a "hidden voice," a tendency to pronounce the printed words silently or even to speak them in a barely audible murmur.
2. The reading is executed from left to right across the page, line by line, until the page is finished. Then, the student moves through subsequent pages using the same line-by-line approach.

Reading that displays these characteristics is sometimes referred to as "subvocal linear" reading, because the words read are sounded in the head ("under the voice") and are read horizontally, line after line.

Observers have documented the subvocal quality of most reading, by interviewing people about what goes on in their minds as they read, and by monitoring the vocal cords during reading. Often, a vibration can actually be detected in the bands of tissue in the larynx as someone reads.

The "linear" feature of most reading becomes evident if you just watch the reader's eyes. The dominant movement of the eyes is almost always the same: left to right, back and forth across the page.

Ultimately, your goal will be to move beyond subvocal linear reading to another approach—what's called the visual-vertical technique. In brief, this kind of reading involves, first, eliminating the silent sounding of the words and replacing it with an exclusively visual perception. Second, it's characterized by a dominant sweep of the eyes vertically down the page, rather than by the usual horizontal, left-to-right movement.

Much of the remainder of this book will be devoted to showing in detail how you can develop the skills that will enable you to become a visual-vertical reader. But for now, just be concerned with the first step—becoming a proficient subvocal linear reader. After you master that skill, you will be in a position to tackle the visual-vertical approach.

Before we go on, let's address a basic question that may have already occurred to you: Once you learn the visual-vertical skill, will you ever have any further use for subvocal linear reading? Or should your goal be to avoid it completely?

Actually, there are a number of ongoing uses for efficient subvocal linear reading, even for those who are experts in the visual-vertical method. Here are some of them:

- *Poetry.* Many times, it's most satisfying to savor the language and rhythms of poems subvocally, rather than to experience them only visually. In fact, it may be best to read the poem out loud, to get the full impact of the writer's genius.
- *Dense textbook material.* If you find you don't have a good grasp of the vocabulary in a particular book or article, you may have to slow down and read line by line to get the full meaning. Concentrated scientific or other technical writing may require analysis and thought as you read—and, therefore, a slower pace.

  (On the other hand, there are many situations in which even the most difficult material is best read quickly, with a visual-vertical approach. For example, it may be helpful first to get an overview of difficult material by reading quickly, and then to return to the hardest passages with a subvocal linear technique.)

21

- *Double-checking.* You may have failed to understand something the author has said. Or you may feel the author made a particularly telling point, or came up with an especially compelling turn of phrase, which bears further scrutiny or meditation.

  In such situations, you'll probably want to return to the section in question and linger over it for a few moments. Most of this type of double-checking or retracing will be done with the subvocal linear approach.

- *Jokes.* To appreciate jokes in a book or magazine—or any other disconnected short anecdotes or aphorisms—it's usually necessary to subvocalize. There's almost no way to get a visual-vertical rhythm going when there's no continuity from one little story or point to the next.

- *Dialogue.* Those who are adept at visual-vertical reading can whip through most novels or plays in record time. But many times, the sensitive, intelligent reader will want to slow down and *hear* the words exchanged between characters. Or he may want to savor a scene.

I recall a confession of sorts by one of the fastest readers I know, Dan Warner, one of our Evelyn Wood teachers. Dan can read many thousands of words a minute, and has frequently demonstrated his skill before audiences in public lectures and on television.

But he also has found a place for subvocal linear reading. For example, he loved reading the *Dune* series of fantasy–science-fiction books by novelist Frank Herbert. With these and other absorbing novels, he'll frequently slow down to about 800–900 words per minute in the last chapter or so to relish the final climax and disposition of the plot–and there's absolutely nothing wrong with that.

This sort of indulgence is perfectly acceptable for a student or anyone else, and will probably enhance one's understanding and enjoyment of many books.

On the other hand, it's a mistake to believe that most books can be enjoyed best at a slower pace. In fact, the emotional impact or intellectual understanding of most passages becomes much stronger with the faster visual-vertical approach. Recall the impression made on the student reading the book about Hiroshima, as described in the opening chapter.

In the last analysis, of course, selecting between these two approaches is a judgment call *you* must make for yourself. A rule of thumb I've found helpful is this: If for some reason, the sound of the words seems particularly important, then it's probably a good idea to revert to the subvocal approach. But if your main objective is to absorb the meaning of the passage as effectively as possible, the visual-vertical approach will be more appropriate.

## How to Fine-Tune Your Hidden Voice

Subvocal linear reading is clearly an important part of your repertoire of reading skills. Becoming proficient in this slower-paced technique will increase your reading speed far beyond its present rate and is an essential first step in Mentally Soaring with visual-vertical reading.

But how exactly do you fine-tune this skill?

First, it's important to evaluate accurately, in hard, clear terms, just how fast you can expect to read using the subvocal linear approach. Second, you must learn to anticipate and overcome the speed plateaus you'll encounter periodically as your reading speed increases.

Specifically, as you develop your subvocal linear skills, you may expect to move through these levels:

- *200–400 words per minute.* In this speed range, you are reading rather inefficiently. There are periodic or frequent regressions, where you stop and look back over material you've already supposedly read. Your mind tends to wander, and your concentration is relatively poor.
- *400–600 words per minute.* At this plateau, your subvocal linear reading has become more efficient. You regress infrequently, if at all, and are most likely making good use of the simple underlining hand motion to pace yourself. (I'll describe this technique shortly.)
- *600–900 words per minute.* This is the highest possible speed for those using the subvocal linear approach. It does represent a significant level of achievement. At this level you do not regress; your concentration is high; and your underlining hand motions and horizontal, linear eye movements are operating at their top level of efficiency.

About 900 words per minute is the absolute maximum speed a student can hope to reach by using the subvocal linear technique. In a sense, this speed represents a kind of "sound barrier" for speed reading. To break through it, you need to employ different tools and techniques. It's at this point that visual-vertical reading and other, more sophisticated study strategies and hand motions become necessary.

On the other hand, although there is an outside limit to this subvocal, "subsonic" kind of mental flight, those who have perfected this technique really do seem to untrained readers to be whizzing quickly through the printed page.

The difference between this top subvocal linear plateau and the average student's reading speed is startling in many ways.

Think about it for a moment: A person reading a 90,000-word book at 900 words per minute would finish in 100 minutes, or an hour and forty minutes. By contrast, a student reading at the average of 250 words per minute would take 360 minutes, or six hours.

So if you never move through the 900-word-per-minute barrier, you'll still be in much better shape than if you stay at your present level. On the other hand, I can promise you that you will crash through that subvocal barrier into the realm of Mental Soaring—*if* you first learn the basics of subvocal linear reading, and then try the visual-vertical approach.

Now, what are these basics that can turn you into a highly efficient subvocal linear reader and move you up toward the 900-word-per-minute barrier?

The tools and techniques you'll need are basically quite simple. I've already referred to them briefly in the first chapter and encouraged you to begin using them, as I expect you're doing right now. In more detail, here are the basics I've already introduced, along with some new tips and techniques:

**Be sure you can see the page.** This may seem an all-too-obvious point, but you'd be surprised at the number of people who have to hold reading matter at arm's length, or right under their noses, in order to read. It's absolutely essential to wear properly prescribed glasses if you need them. If you don't have the right prescription, you'll automatically be limited in how efficiently or quickly you can read.

This reminds me of a student who was farsighted in one

eye and nearsighted in the other. Without glasses, he could read with his nearsighted eye, but the words were unintelligible to his farsighted eye.

Unfortunately, he spent months trying to struggle along, reading with his one good eye—until he finally decided to have an eye exam and buy some glasses. With corrected vision, he found that his reading speed and endurance increased dramatically.

**Select a quiet, comfortable environment.** To reach your full potential, you'll need a quiet room or corner, with as few distractions as possible.

Be sure the lighting there is bright, and conducive to easy reading. A dark area makes it necessary to struggle over words that you can't see well. On the other hand, a glaring light, with too much reflection, may make it equally difficult to make out words and can induce headaches.

Finally, it's absolutely essential to have a solid, firm writing surface on which to jot down notes. As we move further into developing your study techniques, you'll discover that the drafting of a "recall pattern," or note outline, is an essential part of the learning process. But to take efficient notes, you must have a desk or table that makes writing an easy and comfortable experience.

Choose a chair that's comfortable but upright. Reclining as you read makes it hard to handle the book efficiently, and creates terrible problems as you try to take notes. Also, leaning back too much or lying down just encourages most of us to nod off.

As we reviewed these points in one class, a student objected, "Studying is unpleasant enough—at least let me relax while I'm reading!" But on analyzing the situation, she discovered that even though she was getting plenty of rest, including a number of naps during her study period, she was spending about twice as long as necessary covering the assigned material. Simply shifting to another, more upright chair immediately cut many minutes off her study time.

**Break your book in.** Certain mechanical considerations are extremely important in increasing your reading speed, and one of the most important is preparing a book so that it's easy to handle.

Breaking in makes page-turning much easier and also helps preserve the book in good condition. It's essential, especially when the student moves into very high-speed reading, for the book to lie flat on the desk or in the hands, and for the pages to turn easily. Otherwise, you may inadvertently cut hundreds of words per minute off your reading speed.

To break in a book, place it on your desk or another flat surface so that it rests on its spine, on the binding. Then open both the front and back covers slowly, until they rest flat on the table. (Continue to hold up the pages of the book, at right angles to the table.) Allow a few pages from each side of the book to flop down toward the desk, and run your thumb or a finger down the inner margin, against the inner binding, to flatten the pages out. Continue this flattening process until the entire book is open on the table, parted approximately midway through the pages. Then flip through the the upper and lower corners of the pages of the book, as you would through a deck of cards, to make them more flexible for page-turning.

**Become an active page-turner.** Efficient page-turning is a major mechanical tool for moving into the upper ranges of speed reading.

The first thing you should do to become an efficient

page-turner is assume an active attitude. The best readers are participatory readers who get deeply involved in moving through printed matter. They design their own learning framework and set up the best structures for assimilating and using new information. They establish the pace at which they want to move through printed material, and in general, orchestrate their own learning process.

Essential to the establishment of a good pace for studying is learning how to turn pages effectively. To become an active page-turner, first sit up straight, with your feet flat on the floor. When you slouch, you become less alert and therefore less involved with your studies. On the other hand, sitting up straight and choosing the rate at which you'll turn the pages encourages participation and enhances concentration.

What is the best technique for turning pages?

A right-handed student will usually pace himself with his right hand. So most often, it's best for right-handers to turn pages with their left hand.

We've found it's best for right-handers to place the book flat on the table and wrap their left forearms and hands around the top or back of the book, so that the fingers of the left hand rest easily at the top right corner of the book. The index finger of the left hand should snuggle just under the page at the upper right-hand corner. Applying slight pressure with the other left-hand fingers against the top right-hand pages should cause the pages to lift up slightly so that you can insert your index finger under the first one.

With your left hand and index finger in this position, you're poised to flip the page over slightly just as you finish reading the bottom part of the right-hand page. *Important:* Your page-turning hand and finger should always be in position by the time you've reached the middle of the right-hand page in your reading.

Then, when you finish the page and have turned it, once again position your left hand and index finger so that you're ready for the next page turn.

A different approach is necessary for left-handers. The left-hander should pace himself with his left hand and let his right hand do the page-turning. But the left-hander should usually hold the book at the base of the spine with his right hand and then also use his right hand to turn the pages from the *bottom* of the book.

Of course, none of these page-turning positions or techniques represents a hard-and-fast rule that you must follow. They are only suggestions. The important thing is for you to find the position that is most comfortable for you and that enables you to turn the page most easily and quickly, with a minimum of shifting or movement.

**Use the underlining hand motion.** The underlining hand motion involves just what its name implies: You move your hand from left to right across the page under the line of type you're reading, as though you were drawing a line underneath the words.

The purpose of this technique is threefold:

First, the motion helps you coordinate your eye movements with your hands at a predetermined pace as you read. This skill becomes increasingly important later as you learn other, more complex hand motions.

Second, the steady underlining motion helps keep your eyes from stopping on single words or terms in the text.

Third, the motion keeps you moving forward in the text and minimizes or eliminates regression.

The explanation below assumes a right-handed reader, who will typically use his right hand to execute the movements. Left-handers should follow the same procedures with their left hands.

- Place your right hand palm-down on the page, with the thumb against or folded under the palm.
- Relax your fingers and spread your hand out fairly flat on the page.
- Move the tips of your fingers along smoothly across the page, just under the line you're reading.
- At the end of the line, lift your fingers about a quarter-inch to a half-inch above the page, and then bring your hand back diagonally down to the beginning of the next line. *Don't skip any lines.*
- Repeat this procedure down the page.

**Don't regress as you read.** Assuming an active approach toward reading and using the underlining hand motions will minimize a tendency to read back over material you've already covered. Sometimes you'll feel you've missed something, and the temptation to reread a passage will become almost overwhelming. Resist it!

Believe me, there will be plenty of opportunity to go back over a passage at the end of a study or reading session if you feel you have to. Almost always, however, you'll find yourself picking up material later in the text that you think you've missed. Or you may find that the material wasn't that important after all.

Most people read as slowly as they do because they allow themselves the luxury of a wandering mind or an undisciplined, regressing approach to reading. This leads to the habit of rereading and to very low reading speeds. But if students don't allow themselves this luxury, they can break the bad habit—and their reading speeds will begin to soar.

Also, a pervasive fear that they're going to miss something essential grips most readers. As a result, they read, and reread, and *re*reread in an effort to pick up everything.

Unfortunately, this approach actually tends to reduce comprehension and understanding, rather than improve them. Most studies confirm that moving along swiftly and systematically, with little or no regression, enhances comprehension. Nothing that's important will be missed with this approach, and steady reading makes it easier to understand the flow and continuity of the text. But to believe this fact, it's necessary to put aside fear and venture forth into the untested waters of faster, more efficient reading.

Fear is a theme that will emerge again and again in these pages. For example, when readers begin to try their wings beyond the 900-word-per-minute barrier with visual-vertical techniques, they typically become anxious. They say to themselves, "How can I possibly read this way? I won't retain or understand a thing!"

If this sounds like you, don't worry. With practice, you'll learn there's no reason for fear, other than the fact that you're delving into the unknown. When you become more familiar and comfortable with the new techniques, the fear will disappear.

The same is true of regressive reading. You may hold onto your safety net—rereading—out of concern that you'll miss something important. But if you throw that net away, you'll find your comprehension actually increases, and your speed increases dramatically, too.

To illustrate what I mean, let's try another reading test. You've been using basic hand motions and some of the other tools I described in chapter one. Now—in perhaps the only major exception I'll ever make to my no-regression admonitions—I want you to go back to page 17 and reread the list of techniques for efficient subvocal linear reading. In particular, be sure that you're in a comfortable position; that you're turning pages efficiently; and that you're using that underlining hand motion, with no regression.

———

Now for the test. Have a pad and a pencil nearby. Look at your watch with the second hand and note on the pad the exact minute and second. BEGIN READING NOW. I'll stop you at some point later in the text so that you can see how your reading speed has improved.

## Those Remarkable Mini-Lessons

Many parents have been deeply impressed by what happens in the "mini-lessons" at our learning centers, where they observe their children being introduced to the Evelyn Wood method of study. In the typical mini-lesson, which involves one forty-five-minute session with an instructor, the students receive various kinds of reading material and are asked to read it as fast as they can. Then, they calculate their reading speed.

Next, the instructor gives several short talks, describing techniques that will improve the students' reading speed. These include previewing the material in advance of regular reading; using special hand motions; developing the discipline to not read back over material already covered; and reading the material by looking at groups of words, rather than at each word individually.

Finally, at the end of the session, the instructor asks the students to apply what they've learned by giving them another test. Consistently, the students show an average increase in their reading speed of 50 percent, with improved comprehension.

Even more dramatic from the parents' vantage point, however, is what they observe during the final test. As the students apply their techniques and work at increasing their reading speed, parents notice that the instructor begins to cavort at the front of the room. He may pick up a chair and hold it over his head, do pirouettes like some awkward ballet dancer or otherwise act outrageously within a few feet of the students.

But amazingly, none of the youngsters even notices. They are concentrating so hard on their reading that they become oblivious of what's going on around them.

Most of the parents have never seen their children pay such close attention to their reading. Usually, after this presentation the adults are completely sold on the reading and study concepts they've seen demonstrated. They realize that by encouraging these and similar study techniques at home, it's possible to transform their children's study habits, concentration and academic performances.

I've seen much the same thing happen with a group of adults who take a mini-lesson. In one urban high school, the teachers were periodically given part of a workday to explore ways to further their own education. As part of this program, they invited a team from our Evelyn Wood organization, including the topflight instructor Dan Warner whom I've already mentioned, to show them how speed reading works.

It was fairly obvious that this group, which was noisy and restless, was going to be difficult to reach. But Dan has encountered plenty of bored and skeptical audiences before—and he's also had plenty of experience cutting through their negativism and getting them interested and involved.

The first thing he did was initiate a dialogue with them: "Have any of you ever heard of us?" he asked.

A number indicated they had.

"I understand you work with youngsters and are interested in getting them to learn more efficiently, with greater levels of concentration—is that fair?"

"Yes," the class responded in unison. Almost immediately, he had them with him, interacting constructively and anticipating with some interest what he was going to say or do next.

"Mind-wanderers, are you here today? Do any of you ever have trouble concentrating on what you're reading or studying? Do you ever fall asleep when you read?'"

"No!" they all said loudly—with big grins that showed they meant the opposite.

"Procrastinators, are you here?" Dan continued. "That's where I came from. I took this course back in 1967, when I was in grad school. But I had had plenty of problems before that. At the end of two years of undergraduate school, I flunked out because I kept putting my work off. I took notes like a crazy fool in classes, but then, I'd wait until the night before the test to read and study the material."

But Dan did manage to finish college; he went on to graduate school; and he took the Evelyn Wood dynamic reading course. "I proceeded to *nail* the next tests I took in grad school," he told the class. "In fact, I became so adept at reading that the Evelyn Wood people asked me to teach."

After finishing his preliminary remarks, Dan passed out copies of Albert Camus's novel *The Stranger* and said, "Now I want to find out how fast you can read."

He had them read, beginning on page 1, for two minutes. Then, he stopped them and showed them how to calculate their reading speed. Most were in the 200-to-300-word-per-minute range.

"But you know what?" Dan said. "Any darned fool can read one thousand to three thousand words per minute— and you can too if you just learn to operate a little differently than you do now. So let me explain exactly how to do it."

Needless to say, by then you could have heard a pin drop in that class. Dan went on to give more background on the Evelyn Wood Program and to provide an overview of the lesson plan. He introduced them to the concept of using hand motions and showed them the simple underlining hand motion that I've already explained. At first, he instructed them just to relax and move their hands smoothly back and forth without trying to read.

He suggested that they try the motion at different speeds, including the fastest movements they could manage "without breaking your fingernails or causing blisters." Next, he asked them to slow way down so that they could see all the words as they moved along; but still, they were not to worry about trying to read.

Now, it was time to increase the speed again. "Press the accelerator a little," he said. "Move those subvocal linear speeds up to four, five, six hundred words a minute. But *don't read.* All right, now really step on it! Get that speed going really fast again, a light, bouncy rhythm. Underline quickly, without reading, but keep your hand and eye movements under control. Be sure your head doesn't begin to swing back and forth. Move your arm and hand easily at the elbow. Keep it loose and relaxed."

Finally, Dan told them to stop. "You've got the idea," he said. "Let's try something a little different. I want you to begin moving that hand back and forth in a fast underlining motion, but again, without reading. Gradually, slow down your hand motion until reading begins to take place.

"Now, turn to the beginning of chapter two. I'm going to time you again for two minutes. This time, I want you to use that underlining hand motion at the speed you determined was comfortable for reading. No faster, and no slower. Ready? Begin."

For two minutes, the class became absorbed in *The Stranger*. Then Dan had them calculate their speeds again. The improvements were dramatic. Many had doubled their rate or were moving along at an even faster clip.

Why did their speeds improve?

As Dan explained, there were a number of contributing factors: first, they weren't rereading; second, they were attacking the book actively with those hand motions, not just sitting still, languidly slipping into a leisurely pace; and third, the hand motions helped them concentrate more completely than before.

"Let me ask you a couple of questions before we wrap this up," he said. "First, how many of you found that during those two minutes you momentarily lost your concentration, or your mind temporarily wandered?"

Nearly everyone's hand went up.

"Of *course* you did!" he responded. "I lose concentration periodically. We all do. But what happened when your mind began to wander? You noticed that you were just wiggling your hand, just moving it along across the page without reading. So you came to your senses and started reading again. The hand motion enhanced your concentration.

"Now, let me ask you a final question: Can any of you tell me what I was doing while you were reading?"

No one could, so Dan said, "Let me show you what I was doing."

He proceeded to spin like a dancer, balance a garbage can on his head, make childish faces and clown around in other ways.

"You didn't see that, did you?" he asked. "Wouldn't you

like to have that kind of concentration every time you sat down to read or study? Wouldn't you like your students to have that kind of concentration? Anyone with a fourth-grade reading ability can."

Even introductions like this can increase reading speeds immediately by at least 50 percent and often much more. Furthermore, people become motivated to learn the more advanced techniques that will propel them to ever higher rates of reading and studying—in short, to the realm of Mental Soaring.

To introduce you to the next step in this process—to the higher speed plateaus, well beyond the 900-word-per-minute subvocal barrier—let's take a brief look at the experience of the founder of this program, Evelyn Wood herself.

## The Evelyn Wood Story

Evelyn Wood began her career as a counselor for girls at a high school in Salt Lake City. As it happened, none of the youngsters she was trying to help could read well, and good reading seemed the key to getting them back on track in their studies. So Evelyn established a remedial reading program.

That program was quite successful, but she wanted to do more. She was especially interested in finding ways that students could read beyond what many experts then regarded as the outer limit of reading speed, 1,000 words per minute. But first, she needed some proof that high-speed reading really was possible. The evidence came unexpectedly from one of her professors, Dr. C. Lowell Lees, the chairman of the speech department at the University of Utah.

Evelyn turned in an eighty-page term paper to Dr. Lees, expecting him to read it at home and return it to her later, as most professors did. Instead, he took the paper from Evelyn and began reading it right there. He went through the entire paper in under ten minutes, graded it and handed it back to her as she sat watching in total amazement.

Furthermore, he had really *read* the material. She found in their ensuing conversation that he was completely familiar with the content, the arguments and the flaws in her work.

How fast had Dr. Lees read the paper? By Evelyn's calculations, he had moved through it at about 2,500 words per minute.

Evelyn now had living proof that the printed word could be read at high speeds, well beyond the generally assumed 1,000 words per minute. But how did Dr. Lees do it? She couldn't figure out his technique, if he had one, even after observing him closely and questioning him.

As she delved further into this subject, however, she became even more convinced that this extraordinary reading rate could be learned and taught. She discovered accounts of Teddy Roosevelt, for example, who was said to read up to three books a day during his presidency. The nineteenth-century British utilitarian philosopher John Stuart Mill was reported to have been able to read as fast as he could turn the pages of a book.

According to one report, Mill had begun reading extensively as a preschooler. Through his formative years, his father, a college professor, would give him a book and tell him to go into another room for a short time and read it. Mr. Mill would then call John back to discuss what he had read.

Obviously, there was tremendous pressure on young John to concentrate and move quickly through the assigned material. By this "on-the-job training," he soon developed into a highly skilled, extremely fast reader.

But even after investigating these and other reputed speed readers, Evelyn still couldn't come up with a technique that could be taught to slow readers. Was high-speed reading and learning an unteachable skill that only a few naturally adept individuals could master?

Next, Evelyn Wood launched a search for the fastest readers alive. She eventually found fifty-three people who could read from 1,500 to 6,000 words per minute. But even after interviewing them and observing them closely, she couldn't identify a common technique.

To be sure, all their eyes moved quickly, and they traveled in one dominant direction, vertically down the page. But *how* did they do it? she asked, increasingly frustrated.

One fall day in 1958 she sat by the side of a brook reading *Green Mansions,* by W. H. Hudson. She was reading fairly quickly, but at nothing near the speeds of the best readers she had observed and read about.

Finally, in utter frustration, she threw the book across the water and just sat there, thoroughly annoyed and stymied. A short time later, realizing that this mood wasn't getting her anywhere, she waded through the water, retrieved the book and headed back toward the cabin where she was spending her holiday.

That evening, she picked up *Green Mansions* again and was able to enter the mood of the story more easily. Some dirt remained on the pages from the rough treatment she had given the volume earlier, and as she read she started brushing the dirt away with the side of her hand.

Suddenly, she was moving through the pages at high

speed, as her eyes followed her hand's natural, relaxed brushing movements. Before she knew it, she had read more than 50,000 words in less than ten minutes—or a rate of nearly 5,000 words per minute!

From this experience was born the basic Evelyn Wood method of reading at high speeds by using the hand as a pacer. Over the next two years, Evelyn fine-tuned her technique in a speech and reading course she taught at the University of Utah. In 1959 she established the first Evelyn Wood Reading Dynamics Institute in Washington, D.C., and the rest is history.

Obviously, what I call Mental Soaring has been around for a long time. Also, small numbers of people in recent generations have discovered the high-speed approach on their own. But it was only in 1959 that the techniques became available to the public through the Wood courses, and now, we're taking the next step: bringing all the specifics of that program to you through this book.

—

STOP READING NOW and look at your watch. Record the precise time. Then, using the method described on page 16, calculate your reading speed. Assume that you've read 2,450 words.

My guess would be that you've improved your reading speed significantly. In any case, keep reading and learning, and your pace will continue to quicken.

—

In this chapter, you've begun to get off the ground in your reading. You're in the air and probably moving at faster speeds than you ever dreamed possible. But another barrier, the 900-word-per-minute limit, remains to be broken. Let's get started on that goal next.

## *ACTION DIGEST*

*1.* The maximum speed for subvocal linear reading is about 800–900 words per minute.

*2.* Subvocal linear reading can best be used for poetry, dense textbook material, double-checking, jokes, and dialogue.

*3.* These are the basics of all efficient reading:

   a. Be sure you can see the page.

   b. Select a quiet, comfortable environment.

   c. Break in your book.

   d. Become an active page-turner.

   e. For the best subvocal linear reading, use the underlining hand motion.

   f. Don't regress as you read.

# 3

# *Mapping Out Your Academic Flight Plan*

The fastest, most efficient reading or studying begins with a specific purpose. Conversely, trying to read or study without a goal in mind will make learning more difficult.

If you try to take in information at random, without any objectives to guide you, several things will happen: You'll become disorganized; you'll probably become confused; and you'll most likely retain little or any of the material— or you'll spend inordinate amounts of time memorizing disconnected bits and pieces of information that you barely understand.

Yet when a purpose is present, this bleak picture changes dramatically for the better. Suddenly, the door swings open to the possibility of *supersonic* reading and learning.

Why are goals and objectives so important for fast and efficient learning?

Establishing a goal at the very beginning of a learning session will enhance your ability to recall key points and concepts. Also, if you make the goals personal and interesting for yourself, you'll tend to become more emotionally involved in the subject matter—and your ability to remember what you study will increase dramatically.

How does this work?

Memory experts have found that having a definite set of goals or questions about study materials gives the student a hook on which to hang new information. This beginning reference point helps launch the all-important, memory-promoting process of developing associations and links between different facts and concepts. It's much easier to remember a series of related things than a list of unrelated items.

Furthermore, adding an emotional element (such as humor or deep concern) can enhance the student's ability to recall material later.

Suppose you've been assigned some materials on ozone-related threats to the environment. If you've been reading the newspapers, you may know that there are at least two different kinds of problems with ozone: one from ozone-polluted air at ground level, and another from damage to the ozone layer in the upper atmosphere.

Now, instead of just starting to read your materials on ozone-related problems without any particular viewpoint, pose a few specific questions: "What are the sources of air pollution by ozone? What, if anything, can we do about this problem? Does it pose any major danger to humanity in the short term, or do we have some time to solve it? Am I in any danger?"

Then, as you move into the other challenge presented by ozone—i.e., the "rip" in the upper atmosphere—you might ask another series of detailed and personal questions: "How long has the problem existed? What's caused it? Am I doing anything to aggravate this threat? What function does the ozone layer serve? What's the danger to animal and plant

43

life on earth? What diseases may members of my family face? What can I do to help solve this problem?"

Asking these questions will establish links and associations between different facts and concepts. As a result, the information you read will be more firmly impressed on your memory.

Also, having a goal will increase the speed at which you can go through new material. By formulating a specific objective for reading at the outset of a study session, you'll be more motivated and focused, and you'll tend to search avidly through the text, trying to find the information that fulfills your objective.

Although the best students often use some form of this goal-oriented, question-asking approach, most average students skip this step. The average person, for instance, might begin a text assignment on the history of the Civil War battle of Gettysburg by starting aimlessly from the first paragraph without having any well-formed purpose in mind. Or if they do have a goal, it's most likely very general: for example, "I want to learn about this battle."

A trained, "supersonic" reader, in contrast, will initially pose specific questions with a definite learning goal in mind: Who were the generals who led the Union and Confederate troops? How many military engagements occurred —and how devastating were they? What was the turning point of the battle? What was the significance of the battle in view of the Civil War as a whole?

If you think about it, you'll realize that no special knowledge is required to formulate such queries. You can come up with the questions and goals you need simply by drawing on your general store of information, or by glancing over the jacket copy, cover or introduction of the book. Then, as you read, you'll be inspired to ask other, more detailed questions.

Unfortunately, though, few students have any specific objectives in mind when they begin to read academic materials. Or at best, any goals they do have tend to be hopelessly vague or general. When asked what they're trying to accomplish in their reading, they answer: "to learn what I need to know for the test," or "to find out what this author has to say."

The best students, however, set much more specific objectives. With fiction, for instance, they may ask before they begin to read, "Who is the main character? What is he or she trying to do? When are the events taking place? Where are they occurring? How are the characters trying to achieve their ambitions or aspirations?"

Then, as they read, they'll seek answers to their preliminary questions. In addition, they'll begin to formulate additional questions, which ask for more and more detailed information. For example: "Now that I know the main characters are Tom and Gail, what is the relationship between them? Do they like each other? Hate each other? Do they have similar goals? If so, how are they working together to accomplish them? If their goals are in conflict, how does the resulting clash between the characters further the plot?"

Setting a purpose for reading by asking preliminary questions "revs up" the thinking process and helps increase reading speed and recall ability.

———

But something else is required to assist the mind to recall important information—and that is superior note-taking skills.

First of all, the best students are fast at note-taking. They can sail along in their reading with a pencil in hand, jotting down central facts and ideas with hardly a break in stride.

Second, the notes they take are clear, comprehensive and well-organized enough to be used weeks or months later as an aid to recalling information essential for a test.

What promotes insightful questions and accurate note-taking? It all begins with the kind of study space you establish.

## Your Own Special Study Space

John, a very bright fifteen-year-old, consistently scored a B-minus or lower on his tests at school, even though he claimed to spend several hours a day in study.

When a counselor evaluated John's methods, however, she discovered that he studied in environments that worked against effective reading and note-taking. In the first place, John spent several hours a week in the company of his girlfriend while "studying." Predictably, he accomplished very little. On one such occasion, for example, he covered only five pages in a history text during a two-hour period, and he could remember practically nothing of what he read.

Second, John devoted an hour a day to "studying" in the school library. But in those sessions, he was halfheartedly trying to read or work at a large common table, where jokes were constantly cracked, notes were passed around and other distractions got in the way.

Third, during the few hours he managed to work at home, John either opened his books in front of a television set or in the presence of loud rock music. Consequently, the boy made little headway in his assignments.

The only time John really began to *move* with his reading was just before his exams, when the pressure was on and the fear of failure loomed large. Because he was intelligent, he managed to cram enough information into his head at the last minute to pass, and sometimes he even scored in the low honors category. But he never reached his full academic potential.

The first corrective step for John, as for any other mediocre student who wants to make it to the top, was to find a better study space. He needed a well-equipped, comfortable "cockpit" which would allow him to do his job without unnecessary distractions. A pilot confronted in his working environment with as many interruptions and distractions as John faced probably would have lost control of his craft, and might have crashed.

In the previous chapter, we've already considered some of the important ingredients of an effective study space. A good place to study becomes even more essential for those who hope to hit the fastest academic speeds. So let's consider in greater detail what space needs the best students typically require for top performance.

**A quiet, secluded table or desk.** The greatest sustained speeds in study—and often the most successful academic performances—are usually achieved by students who prepare in some degree of seclusion.

This doesn't mean that you have to be completely isolated, out of sight and sound of other students. When siblings are around at home or classmates are in libraries or study halls, total isolation may be impossible.

But still, with a little effort it's always possible at least to find a semisecluded spot. In the library, for example, our best students usually try to find the table, desk or carrel farthest from the "action," the socializing and horseplay that often exist in any school setting.

What about the fear that such an approach to study may seem antisocial?

At some point, the serious student has to make a decision about priorities. Let's face it, you only have a limited amount of time each day. Extra study time at school can be a real gift for those who want to do well academically and have some time for extracurricular activities. In the long run, those who study when the time is available, and play when study is finished—and do well in both—will gain the respect of most of their classmates.

Some of these same considerations may apply at home, where there are brothers or sisters, or where living space is limited. But most good students manage to find quiet times and places at home, and when they do, they take full advantage of them.

**A study space devoted entirely to the task at hand.** For many people, a desktop cluttered with extraneous items, unrelated to the designated job, makes it much harder to concentrate.

If a girl has a couple of her basketball trophies or a picture of her boyfriend in front of her, she's more likely to fantasize about basketball or her boyfriend than to study.

Or suppose she's studying math, but her history and English homework is piled underneath. In such a case, it's easy to lose the math materials in the academic "archeological dig" on the desk. Speed and efficiency become impossible if the physical environment works against them.

A study area should be devoted entirely to study, if that's possible. And when one subject has been completed, you should remove the materials and then store or file them so that the study space is clean and ready for the next project.

**Good lighting and furniture.** I've already mentioned this point in some detail in the previous chapter, but let me reemphasize one thing: If you can't see your study materials clearly, or if you are distracted by an uncomfortable chair or a rickety table, your ability to reach high reading speeds will be seriously limited.

**Assemble all necessary study materials before you begin.** There's nothing more disruptive to efficient learning than constantly having to rummage around to find pencils, paper or text materials that you forgot to lay out on your desk.

To help with this process, you will do well to write down a brief list of the required materials for a study session before starting. Then, when these things are assembled in plain sight, you can proceed with the assurance that you have at hand *all* the basic items necessary to do your best work.

This procedure is especially important for those who are about to leave home and head for the library. If you get to the library but then find you've left a needed book or a pen and pencil at home, the urge to study that day may vanish entirely.

**Soft background noise or music may be helpful.** Some people prefer total silence when they study, but unfortunately, this sort of quiet is hard to find anywhere, except perhaps in a soundproof chamber. As a result, I recommend reading and studying in a spot where there is steady, soft background noise, such as traffic or soothing instrumental music. This kind of unobtrusive sound often helps absorb and mask more disturbing sounds, such as honking horns or occasional loud voices.

Some studies have suggested that certain types of instrumental music can actually help readers pace themselves and concentrate better. This is an individual matter which you must work out for yourself.

On the other hand, it's important to avoid noise that distracts, such as loud music or any other recordings that tempt you to listen or sing along. Another offender is television, which engages the eyes as well as the ears.

In any case, remember that your main purpose is to promote reading and learning speed and efficiency; so if background music helps, fine. But if every type of recording you try seems to work against your main purpose, stay away from them.

When you have your special space in order, the next important consideration is the management of time.

## Traveling in Time

### The Term or Quarterly Schedule

It's important to design a long-term study schedule, which should cover the entire quarter or semester. To set up such a plan, a sample of which appears on page 52, it's necessary to ascertain all the important dates on the academic calendar. These include deadlines for papers, scheduled quizzes, times for major tests and oral presentations.

Many people resist keeping lists or writing down appointments. But the most successful people, including the most successful students, are usually ardent list-makers and schedule-keepers. I don't know of any top executives who fail to keep some sort of daily schedule diary or "to do" list!

Yet many students are just as busy as high-ranking corporate executives or professional people. In fact, right now may turn out to be the busiest time of your life, if you're an active, ambitious student. Trying to juggle study assignments, tests, term papers *and* one or more extracurricular activities *and* a regular social life can seem overwhelming—

especially to the disorganized. So it's essential for you to learn the art of devising and sticking to a written personal schedule.

Some of the most frustrating times of my own life have been the few times when I've failed to record an appointment or a deadline. On those occasions, I've sometimes found to my chagrin that a project I've forgotten about is due, or an important person I had planned to meet has been left stranded.

It only takes one or two such embarrassments to impress any conscientious person with the fact that written schedules are absolutely essential for a successful, well-ordered life. There's no reason for any student to forget a term-paper deadline, overlook a homework assignment or fail to remember to study for a test. It's just a matter of learning what the key dates and requirements are and then writing them down.

In addition to figuring out the big picture for your academic year, it's also important to draw up a weekly and daily schedule so that studying, leisure activities, meals and extracurricular commitments can be recorded in one place. This way, you will be able to see at a glance exactly where you have to be and what's required of you at a given hour on a given day.

## How to Set Up a Weekly Schedule

As you devise a weekly schedule like the one on page 53, these suggestions should help:

Write your class schedule and other permanent activities in ink. Then fill out the rest of the schedule in pencil, since you may have to make changes as the term progresses.

Insert your mealtimes on the chart. Be sure to allow enough time for a leisurely meal and for travel between the

## Sample Term Schedule

| DATE | MISCELLANEOUS | PAPERS | EXAMS |
|---|---|---|---|
| October 1 | PHYSICAL SCIENCE QUIZ | | |
| October 15 | PHYSICAL SCIENCE QUIZ | | |
| October 29 | | ENGLISH PAPER | |
| October 29 | PHYSICAL SCIENCE LAB. REPORT | | |
| November 12 | | | PHYSICAL SCIENCE MIDTERM |
| November 15 | | | FRENCH MIDTERM |
| November 17 | | | PSYCHOLOGY MIDTERM |
| November 17 | PSYCHOLOGY EXPERIMENT | | |
| November 23 | | HISTORY PAPER | |
| December 3 | PHYSICAL SCIENCE QUIZ | | |
| December 17 | | ENGLISH PAPER | |
| December 17 | PHYSICAL SCIENCE LAB. REPORT | | |
| January 17 | PHYSICAL SCIENCE QUIZ | | |
| Special schedule to be announced/Feb. | | | FRENCH FINAL |
| " | | | PSYCHOLOGY FINAL |
| " | | | ENGLISH FINAL |
| " | | | HISTORY FINAL |
| " | | | PHYSICAL SCIENCE FINAL |
| | | | |

Copyright © 1984 Evelyn Wood Reading Dynamics, Inc.

52

# Sample Weekly Schedule

| | MON. | TUES. | WED. | THURS. | FRI. | SAT. | SUN. |
|---|---|---|---|---|---|---|---|
| 7:00 | Breakfast | Breakfast | Breakfast | Breakfast | Breakfast | Breakfast | |
| 8:00 | FRENCH CLASS | Study History | FRENCH CLASS | Study History | FRENCH CLASS | Study History | |
| 9:00 | Study French | HISTORY CLASS | Study French | HISTORY CLASS | Study French | HISTORY CLASS | |
| 10:00 | PSYCH. CLASS | Study History | PSYCH. CLASS | Study History | PSYCH. CLASS | Study History | |
| 11:00 | ENGLISH CLASS | Study Phy. Sci. | Study Psych. | Study Phy. Sci. | ENGLISH CLASS | | |
| 12:00 | LUNCH | LUNCH | LUNCH | LUNCH | LUNCH | | |
| 1:00 | Study English | PHYSICAL SCIENCE | Study English | PHYSICAL SCIENCE | Study English | | |
| 2:00 | Study Psych. | Study Phy. Sci. | ENGLISH REC. | PHY. SCI. LAB. | Study Psych. | | |
| 3:00 | Study Psych. | | ENGLISH REC. | PHY. SCI. LAB. | Study Psych. | | |
| 4:00 | | P.E. | Study English | P.E. | | | Overall Review of |
| 5:00 | | | Study English | Study Phy. Sci. | | | Week's Work |
| 6:00 | DINNER | DINNER | DINNER | DINNER | DINNER | | DINNER |
| 7:00 | | | | | | | Study Psych. |
| 8:00 | Study English | Study French | Study English | Study French | | | Study French |
| 9:00 | Daily Review | Daily Review | Daily Review | Daily Review | | | |

Copyright © 1984 Evelyn Wood Reading Dynamics, Inc.

53

place where you're eating and your study space or class-room. And remember what your mother probably always told you: Eating regular meals, including a substantial breakfast, is essential for keeping energy levels high for academic work.

Brain work requires adequate calories and nutrients. If you aren't on a proper diet, you'll probably find you lack the ability to work hard and concentrate for sufficient periods of time to get the most out of your studies.

Now, let me provide you with a few more preliminary tips and guidelines that top students have found useful as they plan their study schedules:

**The forty-minute formula.** In drawing up your own term, weekly and daily schedules, it's important to think in terms of forty-minute study blocks. Longer study periods lead to restlessness, cramped bodies and wandering minds. Most students learn and remember at their highest level of efficiency during the first ten and final ten minutes of these forty-minute periods.

As we'll see later, these two ten-minute segments correspond nicely with two important phases of "supersonic" reading: the preview process, which involves getting a grasp on the main ideas and overall flow of the reading material; and the postview phase, which includes final review, note-taking and note-organizing—a process that enables the student to recall the material better at a later time.

**The two-week rule.** Work very steadily and diligently during the first two weeks of the term. This means a minimum of five hours a day, six days a week in study, for a total of at least sixty hours of reading and note-taking during those two weeks.

Using the high-speed reading and study techniques you'll

find in this book, plan to read *all* your basic class assignments during this initial two-week period. Also, you should formulate comprehensive notes—the "recall patterns" I mentioned briefly in the first chapter—on everything that's read. (We'll be going into the recall pattern concept in much more detail in chapter five.) As the term progresses, review and coordinate the reading you've done with relevant lectures and class discussions.

(*Note:* This rule works best with college courses or in schools where the student knows all the reading assignments at the beginning of the term. If your instructor is in the habit of assigning reading in a piecemeal fashion throughout the term—and if you can't get him to give you the requirements in advance—the best alternative approach is simply to read the assignments immediately as they're handed out.) At first glance, this goal may seem impossible, and given your former study and reading methods, it probably is. But with the Evelyn Wood approach, many students find that only *one* week at this pace is sufficient to complete all their term reading assignments. I'm just suggesting two weeks to make things relatively relaxing for you.

One student, for instance, had pushed his average reading speed up to about 1,200 words per minute. But being conservative, he lowered his estimate of his capabilities for this two-week exercise: He assumed that he could manage an average of 1,000 words per minute. Furthermore, he planned to put in the recommended minimum time of sixty hours in the first two weeks.

As he looked over the assigned materials, he saw that he would be responsible for two "big" reading courses, English and history. The three other classes—one foreign language, a math class and a science course—involved shorter but denser texts.

In the English and history classes, he found that the total number of words he had to read during the term was 1.6 million (the equivalent of twenty 200-page books, averaging 400 words per page). At 1,000 words per minute, he figured he could go through this material in 1,600 minutes, or less than 27 hours!

He had allotted a minimum of thirty hours of study for the first week. So he could count on getting through all the reading and initial note-taking on the texts for those two extensive reading courses before the first week of classes was finished—and still have plenty of time for extracurricular activities and relaxation.

He also used his supersonic reading capabilities on the other three courses during the initial two-week period. But the foreign language, math and science classes required him to go through considerably fewer pages than the English and history did. Consequently, he finished the initial once-through reading and note-taking for these three courses by the middle of the second week.

At the same time, however, this student recognized that these other three courses contained exceptionally unfamiliar and complex subject matter. So he knew this initial, once-through reading was just the beginning. He planned to work on some of the more difficult problem solving and other time-consuming projects throughout the term.

**The relaxed study rhythm rule.** In the middle part of the term or quarter—which constitutes most of the weeks in the school year—the student on this program can, in effect, relax into a slow but steady study rhythm. It's hard for many students to believe how easy and enjoyable, yet productive and stimulating, this time of the school year can be, as long as they have observed the two-week rule.

Most students find they can settle into a pace that involves about two to three hours of study a day, five days a week. That means only about 10 to 15 hours of study each week —not an unusually heavy load at all for secondary school or college.

Of course, the amount of time you devote to study can't be determined by some rigid formula. Sometimes you may find that you can do well on less than ten hours a week. Other times, such as just before the deadlines for term papers or midterm exams, you may want to put in more than fifteen hours per week.

Remember, there's a rhythm to study that you should learn to discern and follow for the best results. Also, different courses may impose varying learning requirements that call for different study techniques.

For example, some of your study time will undoubtedly be devoted to memory work—such as learning vocabulary words in a foreign language. It's been suggested that twenty to thirty minutes for one memorizing session is plenty for most students. Any more, and the mind tends to wander.

A memory plan that works for many students: Take about twenty minutes to work on the memory assignment; then take a break or shift to another area of study, such as reading; and finally, come back to the memory work for another twenty-minute session.

Reading literature, on the other hand, can continue for two to three hours at a stretch or even longer if the student remains interested. In general, though, as I mentioned earlier, most experts feel that about forty minutes, with five- to ten-minute breaks between sessions, is the optimum time for study.

What else do the best students do with this relaxed time period in the middle of the term? They commonly follow several study practices:

**They mesh their class sessions and their study.** Because even the best students sometimes have trouble sitting down to work, many find it helpful to use their lectures to warm up for study.

It's always advisable to get involved in the lecture, for example by silently asking yourself questions as the instructor speaks. Also, you might jot down your own thoughts on the subject as you take notes on what the teacher is saying.

But in most cases, listening to a lecture is a more passive, less demanding activity than the really active work required in reading. So why not use the relatively comfortable environment of the classroom to ease into study?

The easiest way to accomplish this is to schedule at least an hour of study immediately after the lecture, or as soon afterward as is feasible. Then, spend the first five to ten minutes reorganizing your class notes from the lecture. The rest of the study time should be devoted to reading about the subject matter of the lecture class and taking notes on the reading.

If the class is a discussion class rather than a lecture, however, you'll want to take a different approach. For one thing, you'll be expected to become much more active in interacting with the instructor. In fact, higher grades often come from high-quality contributions in such classes.

So I suggest that you schedule a study period *before* the discussion class. During that time, review the subject matter that you expect the instructor to be talking about, and also read and study related materials that might be used in the discussion. The preliminary study period, plus the discussion in the classroom, will help burn the subject matter into your memory and should provide positive payoffs later on exams.

Warming up before a discussion class can be especially helpful for language courses. When you're learning a new language, frequent review of vocabulary and grammar is essential in developing facility in oral presentations. By engaging in review before class and then using this material during class, you'll find your knowledge of the new language grows rapidly.

**The best students continue to read optional and background material in their various courses.** The broader your knowledge of a subject, the better you'll tend to do on papers and tests. Also, the extra reading helps put the required reading into a better perspective and firmer intellectual context. The result is improved recall and understanding of the required material.

Also, this supplementary reading will provide you with a head start on doing research for any course papers that may be due.

**The best students reread selected parts of the required assignments, especially those sections that seemed difficult on the first go-around.** During these study sessions, the top students rework their reading notes (recall patterns) and add to them as needed.

Also, they may begin to memorize certain facts, including the spelling of key names and places, the dates of major events and even short quotations. With regard to this last point, a number of students have found that they can make a tremendously positive impression on instructors by slipping in a direct quote, with page references, from an assigned book or article.

**The top learners ask their teachers questions about things they don't understand.** Besides clearing up any confusion, a one-to-one conversation with the person who will be designing and grading your tests can provide other invaluable insights and advantages. A number of students report that they've gained extremely helpful ideas about how the teacher's mind works, and also what to expect on exams. In most cases, giving the teacher a chance to get to know you and to see your interest in the subject can only work to your advantage. Remember, though, that most instructors have more time early in the term than later, when they're preparing exams, or grading exams and papers.

## Tips for Preparing Short Papers

Your written term schedule should alert you to the deadlines for turning in written assignments. To meet these demands, you should begin weeks in advance gathering material for a long paper, and at least one week in advance for a short paper.

Here's a suggested five-day "flash" schedule for preparing those short papers, which will typically run from two to ten typed, double-spaced pages:

**Day 1:** Think through the course material and select a particular theme or topic for your report. Then, gather the books, recall patterns and other notes that relate to that topic and glance through them to refresh your memory. Finally, draft an outline (recall pattern) for the paper.

**Day 2:** Read through your outline again and add or change material as required. Then, write a complete first draft of the paper. If you have access to a computer with a word processing package, use it. This writing tool will be a big help with the first draft and will enable you to make later changes more easily.

But don't expect this draft to be the final one that you'll turn in. Your goal on this second day is just to get the first draft down on paper. There will be plenty of time later to edit and revise.

**Day 3:** Read over the draft, checking closely for correct grammar, clarity of expression and good organization. You might also try reading the paper out loud to yourself. This is a helpful technique for catching awkward phrasing and other mistakes.

Next, type a second draft which includes all your changes. Ask a friend or family member to read over your draft. Then incorporate any valid suggestions you receive and if necessary type another clean copy.

**Day 4:** Read the most recent draft over again and make any other changes that may seem appropriate. It always helps to "sleep on" written material at least one day before turning it in. That way, you can approach it with a fresh, objective eye in your final editing. Type the final draft.

**Day 5:** Turn in the paper.

Maintaining a schedule like this can remove most of the last-minute deadline pressure that makes the lives of so many students miserable. As you can see, most of the work for the paper has been scheduled in the first two days. After that, it's just a matter of fine-tuning the writing—and adding those touches that can make the difference between an A and a B.

## Tips for the Final Two Weeks

Now, we're moving toward the end of the term, when the thoughts of all students turn to final exams. At this point, the best performers become even more focused, and the relaxed rhythm of middle-term study is replaced by increased intensity—though *not* by cramming.

Here are a few tips to guide you in these last two weeks:

**Try to find out what the format of the exam will be and what topics are most likely to be emphasized.** Then direct your study efforts toward responding to the probable questions on the test.

Frequently, the teacher will drop hints, and you should take them quite seriously. Also, you might want to talk with students who have already taken the course to find out what the final exam was like. In some schools, the instructors even make copies of old exams available.

Why is a knowledge of the test maker's style of drafting questions important? For one thing, some instructors frequently repeat their exams' subject matter and even their questions. It's always better to anticipate the question and then prepare an answer in advance than to have to formulate a response under examination time pressures.

Even if you can't anticipate particular questions, many times a test maker will settle into a certain format that you *can* anticipate. For example, one instructor may favor essays, while another likes multiple choice or fill-in-the-blanks. Becoming familiar with the test format can give you an indication of whether you should focus on broad issues and concepts or on specific facts in preparing for the test.

**Rework your recall patterns and other notes you've taken during the school year.** Make them reflect the format and questions you anticipate on the final exam. Granted, you may turn out to be wrong about the test. But just going through your notes in detail and rewriting them will be a valuable exercise in preparing for the exam.

**If you can find some other students with whom you feel comfortable, you might try setting up a study group to go over exam material.** But let me mention two caveats here. First, don't make any such arrangements with students who are mainly interested in partying or chatting, or who are so hopelessly behind in their work that they can't provide helpful contributions. Second, even with a good, productive group of fellow students, you should still concentrate mostly on private study, and limit your group study severely. A couple of hours a week at most is all that's usually needed for this type of joint preparation.

## The Last Three Days

You're in the final hours of exam preparation—but still, *don't cram*. Keep your life as relaxed and calm as possible.

Studying until you're excessively fatigued or sacrificing sleep to get in extra hours with the books will do you more harm than good at this point. Becoming overtired will promote anxiety and even panic, while staying rested and relaxed will help keep you calm and confident.

Remember: With your term-long program, you've already been studying more regularly and efficiently than the vast majority of your fellow students. Now, if you stay rested and relaxed, you'll be in a position to put out maximum effort on the test.

So mark in on your weekly study schedule the number of hours you feel you can comfortably study in these last three days, without getting wiped out. As you study, you will probably want to focus on these areas:

• Facts and concepts you can't recall or understand easily. Really try to nail down these items in the last few days.

- Questions posed in your textbooks. If you haven't answered all of these, try to finish them. These questions may help you organize and assimilate the material better for the test.
- The index and summary paragraphs in the book. You may find points or categories of information here that you've overlooked in your other studying. If so, add them to your recall patterns.
- Stay positive. Don't engage in negative conversations about the upcoming test or anything else. Putting on your favorite music for an hour or so each day may help.

If you tend to be happier and more relaxed in the company of certain friends, make it a point to spend time with them now. Or if you find you can maintain a better attitude when you're alone, avoid other people for these three days.

## *The Last Night*

Continue with your relaxed approach to study, and be sure to get to bed reasonably early. In addition, eat as you normally do, and get some exercise.

As far as the subject matter is concerned, review all your texts, recall patterns, and notes. Go through this material steadily and quickly. What you want now is an overview of all the facts and concepts in the course. This is not the time to try to learn new material. Rather, you should try to obtain a clear picture of how all the parts of the course fit into the whole.

Finally, be sure to arrive at the site of the exam at least fifteen or twenty minutes before it begins. Schedule your breakfast and other early-morning activities so as to leave plenty of time to make it to the test location at a relaxed pace.

—

These time-management considerations should give you an idea of the way your days and weeks should be organized during a typical term. It's only by adjusting your space and time so that they are conducive to speed and efficiency that you can hope to achieve such speed and efficiency.

Now, with your physical environment and personal schedule in order, let's turn to the take-off—the initial phase of high-speed reading and studying that I've called Mental Soaring.

## *ACTION DIGEST*

*1.* Set a purpose for your reading.

*2.* Choose an attractive study space.

*3.* Establish a term or quarterly study schedule.

*4.* Set up a weekly study schedule.

*5.* Observe the forty-minute formula and the two-week rule.

*6.* Follow the relaxed study rhythm rule.

*7.* Understand the five-day technique for writing short papers.

*8.* Know the tips for the final two weeks before exams.

# 4

# *The Takeoff for Rocket-Powered Reading and Learning*

Many people are under some mistaken impressions about the Evelyn Wood approach to reading.

Some, for instance, believe that the Evelyn Wood program simply involves teaching students to widen their peripheral vision beyond normal human capacities and then to increase the speed at which this broader visual path moves down the page.

Others assume that the well-instructed Evelyn Wood student is supposed to plunge into a book and whiz through it once at a phenomenal rate, with superior comprehension.

But such notions at best contain only partial truths about our program.

Those who become adept at supersonic reading *are* able to take in more words at a glance than the average reader. But the space one can focus on in a piece of reading material is relatively fixed: We can only take in the words contained in a circle about an inch and a half in diameter, with the center of the circle being the point where the eyes focus on the page.

In any event, it's fairly easy, with a certain amount of

practice, to begin to read the maximum groupings of words that your eyes can take in during one look. That ability will develop naturally as you begin to use the techniques I'll be describing in the following pages.

It's also certainly true that readers trained in the Evelyn Wood method move their eyes more quickly while reading. But they usually don't go through the material just once. Instead, the foundation for faster, more efficient reading involves several run-throughs with what we call the Multiple Reading Process. Or, perhaps more accurately, this approach might be termed a "multiple-exposure" or "layering" technique for taking in the printed word. (This layering method should be used for all reading you do, including that done in the first two weeks of the term.)

## The Foundations of Layered Reading

To understand how the Multiple Reading Process, or layering technique, works, it's important to recognize four basic principles on which this concept is based:

**Principle 1:** You must learn to see and accept words and phrases out of their normal expectancy order.

To illustrate, suppose you divide this page in half, drawing a vertical line from top to bottom. Then, assume that you subdivide it crosswise. Imagine a series of about four or five parallel horizontal lines across the page, from the top to the bottom. The words on the page will then fall into a series of rectangles.

Start reading by looking first at the words in the upper left rectangle. Then read those in the upper right rectangle; next, move to the words in the second rectangle from the top on the left; and so on, down the page.

Probably, some of you will find you can take in all or most of the words in each rectangle at a glance. But you won't be reading them in the order in which they're written, as you would if you were reading line by line. Furthermore—and most important—while reading this way you *can* comprehend what the writer is saying, even though you're reading the words out of order. In other words, your mind, in taking in information, isn't limited to the order in which words and concepts are arranged on the printed page. You'll find that the author's logic, the literary style and other features of the text come across quite clearly.

The same principle applies when you're reading the words from the bottom to the top of the page, or even when you go through the book backwards, from the last page to the first.

Granted, getting the maximum amount of information through this out-of-order exposure to the words on a printed page does take some practice to perfect. But you'll find that even on the first try, you can pick up an amazing amount of information by using this approach to reading.

Being able to take in groups of words out of their normal order is one of the fundamentals of Mental Soaring. So when you begin to practice reading later in this book, don't be afraid to take the plunge and get used to dealing with the text this way. Becoming more confident with the out-of-order technique will be a big help as you prepare to break through the 900-word reading barrier to very high speeds and rates of comprehension.

**Principle 2:** Accept visual, as opposed to auditory, reassurance as you read.

As you already know, most people read in a linear subvocal fashion, moving through a book line by line and either actually or in their minds sounding out the words. Yet the fastest and most effective readers rely on their vision as their eyes move in a predominantly vertical direction down the page.

To this end, you must be prepared to *believe your eyes alone* when you read. Don't feel you have to test or hear the sound of words or phrases before you can accept them.

An analogy I like involves the way most people look at a painting, a photograph, a clock, a beautiful scene in the country or a human being. When you see a person you know, you don't have to say to yourself, "That's Joe." Instead, you see Joe and you immediately accept the validity of what your eyes have conveyed to you.

It's much the same with visual reading. You must learn to trust your eyes, even though you've been conditioned for years to check or test the words you see by sounding them out in some way in your head.

To apply this principle, I want you to spend about two to four seconds per page just looking at each of the next six pages. As you look, say out loud key words that you see, and ask yourself, again, out loud, some question about those words. It doesn't really matter what words you choose or what questions you ask. The point here is to keep your voice "busy", to remove it from the reading process. But as you talk out loud, don't allow your eye movement to slow down. Continue to move through each page at the two- to four-second pace.

Now, begin this exercise. When you've finished glancing at the following six pages, return to this point in the text.

———

We encourage the "talk-out-loud" technique to help readers become more active in learning. When you begin to engage aggressively with words and phrases, you are more likely to establish specific objectives in your reading, generate more thoughts and move through the material more swiftly and efficiently.

Also, if your voice is engaged during reading, you can't use it, either actually or in your mind, to sound out the words you're reading. Note that it's important to distinguish this talk-out-loud technique from ordinary subvocal reading. In the former, stating occasional key words and asking periodic questions will block most of your ability to sound out the words in the text. In the latter, the tendency is to sound out most or all of the words in the text.

Let's assume you've followed my instructions and talked while allowing your eyes to take in the printed matter at two to four seconds a page. In that case, you'll find that most of what you've assimilated has been through your visual rather than your auditory faculties.

Obviously, you can't use this talk-out-loud technique in many settings because if you try saying key words out loud, you'll disturb everyone within earshot. But you can say key words silently as you read and thus help to short-circuit your need for auditory reassurance about most of what you see.

The more practice you get with this technique, the more confident you'll become in accepting at face value the visual appearance of the words on the page, without any further checking or testing. Then, your speed and efficiency will leap forward significantly.

**Principle 3:** You must learn to read vertically.

The more adept you become at the various techniques of Mental Soaring, the more you'll tend to read down the page rather than across it.

Also, you'll find that you use your peripheral vision more effectively: You'll comprehend increasing numbers of words in that one- to one-and-a-half-inch-diameter circle on the page where your eyes focus. This ability to make better use of peripheral vision will further enhance your ability to move down the page in groups of words, rather than across the page, word by word.

What does it feel like to read vertically rather than linearly? As you looked over this passage using the talk-out-loud technique, your eyes moved mostly down the page. Otherwise, you never would have made it through the page in two to four seconds. So just from that exercise, you've gained some idea of the sensation of reading vertically.

Later, you'll find that you can slow down the pace to about eight to ten seconds a page, and with a vertical eye movement you'll actually be reading every word. Not only that, you'll comprehend more than when you read line by line and spend one to two minutes on the same page. At ten seconds a page, by the way, you'll be soaring along at approximately 2,000 to 3,000 words per minute.

Also, when you tried the talk-out-loud approach, you were most likely making greater use of your peripheral vision. Generally speaking, when we increase our eye speed, we automatically "spread out" our vision to the maximum in an effort to capture all the images we can.

To understand how this works, stop reading for a moment and look up at some object in the room. Focus on a particular point on that object. Even as you bore in on that point, see how many other objects or movements you can take in out of the corners of your eyes. Without moving your eyes from the focal point, you'll find that you can take in countless other images around you—and that's part of what peripheral vision is all about.

Our peripheral vision is so important that in nighttime

training in the military, infantrymen are taught not to look directly at an object if they want to see it more clearly. Various studies and practical experience have shown that many images and movements come across more clearly at night when they are viewed off-center.

As you practice reading with your peripheral vision, you'll find that you have a somewhat similar capacity. By allowing images to come in from all around your central line of vision, you can take in many words and phrases that are off center from your main focus on the page. And the more words you can grasp at a glance, the more quickly you'll move through any text.

**Principle 4:** Understand the gestalt of what you read.

"Gestalt" is a German word meaning the shape, form or basic structure of a thing—in our case, of a book, article or other reading matter. In the Evelyn Wood technique for reading and learning, gestalt refers to the whole of a text, or the big picture of what has to be absorbed by the student.

The main idea is that before beginning to read, you should first get a sense of what the entire book is about. Among other things, you should determine such things as who the author is, the main purpose of the book, the general range of the subject matter or content, the tone or emotional thrust of the work (i.e., the extent to which the author is trying to convey erudition, excitement, passion, or some other emotion or message) and how the book fits into the course as a whole. You can determine the gestalt simply by employing the overview method—the first step of the layering technique.

———

Layering, or the Multiple Reading Process, involves five steps: 1. overview; 2. preview; 3. read; 4. postview; and

5. review. Here, in more detail, is what happens as you move through each step.

**Overview:** This procedure involves looking the entire book over quickly to determine its organization, structure and tone. The main goal is to understand the gestalt—the main thrust or big picture—of the book.

Among other things, you should check what the cover and jacket copy say about the contents and the author. Also, you should see if there's a preface and introduction, and if so, look them over quickly to get the gist of the text. As part of this preliminary perusal, it's helpful to note the identity of the publisher and the date of publication. In addition, the overview should include a look at the table of contents as an aid in determining the organization of the book.

To complete the overview, flip quickly through the pages, at the rate of about one second per page. (For example, with a three-hundred-page book, this part of the overview would take about five minutes.)

During this flip-through, you needn't worry about reading, but should constantly be asking questions of the material:

- How hard is the book to read?
- Is there any special or difficult terminology?
- Is there a glossary? (In technical books or texts that demand an advanced vocabulary, it's important to know if the author has included a glossary. A listing and definition of tough words in the book itself is generally easier to use than a large or specialized dictionary.)
- Do the chapters tend to be short or long?
- Does each chapter have a helpful introduction or sum-

mary? (If so, it would be wise to focus on those sections in later exposures to the material.)
- Does the author pose questions at any point in the text?
- Are there maps, graphs, charts or other pictured materials?
- Does the author use subheadings? (If so, they may act as a useful guide through the text.)

Finally, when you've completed your overview, you should step back and set your goals for further reading. To this end, it's helpful to pose some other pointed questions, such as the following:

- What exactly do you need to learn from the text?
- What are you likely to be tested on (or be required to use for your research paper)?
- How much of the book do you expect you'll be responsible for—e.g., is it a secondary text or the main one your teacher is using?

With a normal-sized book, overviewing will take no more than about five to ten minutes.

**Preview:** Next, go through the reading assignment at the rate of about four seconds per page. During this phase the main goal is to absorb more detail and to begin to draft an outline (a recall pattern, which I'll be describing in detail in a later chapter).

Also, use the preview to divide the chapter into logical segments—a task which should be relatively easy with non-fiction texts, which are usually organized rather clearly. Headings for subsections, items printed in boldface, and other highlighted material can help you identify the basic structure of the text.

For nonfiction texts, it's usually best to preview the book one chapter at a time. Then, you can go back and read that previewed section (as described in the next step) before moving on to preview and read the next part of the text.

In contrast, works of fiction may be previewed and then read in their entirety, without conducting the preview-and-read process chapter by chapter. The same goes for nonfiction assignments that have a single narrative thrust, such as biographies.

(One of the main goals in previewing fiction, by the way, is to identify the characters, setting, time period and general direction of the plot.)

Obviously, going at a fast preview pace (i.e., about four seconds per page) the first time through a text, you can't hope to absorb or even see every word. Instead, you should look for key facts and concepts. Concentrate especially on the introduction, on summaries and on any questions posed in the chapter. The main purpose is to get a fairly good idea of what the chapter is about.

After you've previewed the chapter (or the entire book) quickly draw up a skeletal outline on the main sections and points contained in the material covered. (This outlining technique will be discussed in detail in chapter six.) Then, you're ready to move on to the next step—the actual process of reading.

**Read:** The goal here is to see every word on every page, and to assimilate and record all the essential information you need for taking tests or writing research papers.

First, you should again preview the first main subsection in any nonfiction chapter you plan to read. Then, go back and read that subsection at your fastest comfortable speed. Don't skip anything at this point; you're not just scanning or hopping from key word to key word. (Usually only one preview will be necessary for a novel or short story.)

As you read, you should make light marks in the book margins with a pencil, but don't underline the text. The marks may be simple lines, checks, question marks or other notations to alert you to particularly important or difficult material, appropriate for later study.

We advise against underlining because it can easily get out of hand. You've probably encountered plenty of students who underline practically every word in the text. (In fact, many of us have been such students.) Yet underlining tends to postpone learning and recall, rather than allow you to learn facts and concepts immediately.

Judicious marking, in contrast, helps keep you active and engaged with the text. For example, we recommend that after you have read a section once, you may want to reread it quickly, especially if it contains crucial course material. This time, though, you should focus on the marked sections.

During this rereading, you may concentrate on those passages noted with question marks because they didn't come across clearly the first time through. Or you may want to mull over very important segments that you starred or checked.

I've heard some students object, "But doesn't all this previewing and repreviewing, reading and rereading, take more time than just going through the book once the way I've always done it?"

The answer to this question is emphatically *no*. As you'll see in later examples—and also in your own personal experience employing these principles—the multiple-exposure or layering approach to learning does increase your comprehension of and contact with study assignments. But this approach doesn't take more time; it takes much less.

After you've finished with your reading and feel you've obtained the information and understanding you need, you should fill in extra details in the recall pattern notes. Then, you're ready to postview.

**Postview:** With a nonfiction textbook, the postviewing should be done immediately after reading a chapter. On the other hand, fiction—or nonfiction with a single, strong narrative flow—may be postviewed as a whole.

Postviewing is the time to go over the entire assignment and think through the relationship of each part of the chapter, section or book to the whole. Also, you should make any final changes that seem appropriate on your recall pattern.

**Review:** At regular intervals, preferably about once a week, you should look over your recall patterns and refresh your memory of the material you've read and how it relates to other materials in the course.

As you can see, in the layered approach to study, only a portion of the time is devoted to what we normally think of as "reading." Furthermore, the more a person needs to absorb written material for academic or business purposes, the *less* time he should expect to spend reading. On the other hand a greater proportion of time will be required for overviewing, previewing, postviewing and reviewing.

We suggest these guidelines for time allotment:

When going over material in preparation for an exam, devote equal time to previewing, reading and postviewing. In doing background reading for a research paper, however, it may be best to spend less time in previewing and postviewing—say about a third of the total hours you devote to the entire assignment. The rest of the time, about two-thirds of the total, should involve reading.

In contrast, if you're reading for pleasure, you might spend minimal time in previewing and postviewing a book or article. Almost all of your time would be devoted to reading.

What kind of comprehension can a person expect at each stage of the layered-reading process? Our experts have discovered that there are five levels of comprehension, which correspond roughly to the five phases of the Multiple Reading Process:

**Comprehension Level 1:** In the overview phase, the student recognizes only individual words and isolated concepts. Comprehension during this process is usually about 10–20 percent: that is, a student would be expected to answer correctly only about one to two questions out of every ten on the material.

**Comprehension Level 2:** With a very fast preview—say about two seconds per page—the student can recognize many more facts, including some key phrases and thoughts. He typically picks up enough information to score 20–40 percent on a comprehension test.

**Comprehension Level 3:** With a slower, more careful preview (approximately four seconds per page), the reader grasps meaningful patterns, main ideas and key themes. Comprehension now moves up to the 40–60 percent range.

**Comprehension Level 4:** At a reading pace slightly faster than the level at which the student feels most comfortable, he becomes even more adept at recognizing meaningful patterns, main ideas and themes. Also, he begins to grasp supporting details in the assignment. Comprehension at this level should bring scores of 60–80 percent.

**Comprehension Level 5:** Finally, reading at a fast but comfortable pace, the student takes in all the material needed to do well on a test or to satisfy other academic objectives. Comprehension should be 80 percent or higher.

Furthermore, combining reading with rereading, post-viewing and reviewing helps the student tap his highest academic abilities.

To see how this layered approach to reading and study can work in practice, let me introduce you to Jennifer, a fourteen-year-old who had been assigned a 120-page history book by her teacher.

## How Jennifer Learned to Use Layered Reading

Jennifer listened closely and worked hard in a class she had been taking on the Evelyn Wood approach to study. But like many students we encounter, at first she lacked confidence in applying the techniques to her daily schoolwork.

To put it bluntly, she feared that the new methods she was learning wouldn't really work, even though she had proved an adept reading student who could consistently average more than 1,200 words per minute.

To her, it was one thing to be reading at a much faster pace, with high comprehension, in the special course we were teaching. It was quite another to try to make the transition with these techniques to an ordinary classroom. Jennifer worried that in practice, in the real world of junior high schools tests and grades, she would fall flat on her face —and fail to measure up academically.

Then, the academic pressure began to increase. She was assigned a 120-page history text on top of other heavy homework assignments, and her teacher said the class could expect a quiz on the book on Monday. That meant she now had two quizzes and a paper deadline for the beginning of the week.

Jennifer realized that if she continued with the slow, pre-Wood way she normally used to read and study, she would be hopelessly overloaded. Yet because she was a serious student and preferred to play it safe in her effort to maintain a high grade-point average, she believed she had only one option. "I'll just have to skip the football game this weekend and cancel some other activities," she sighed. "Otherwise, I'll never finish all my classwork."

Jennifer's Wood instructor, learning of her dilemma, suggested that now might be the ideal time to take the plunge. "Why not take a chance and see if the high-speed approach to learning is really usable for you?" he suggested. "What have you got to lose? Today's Tuesday. Try going through this new book and your other assignments before your Friday game and your other weekend activities. If you make it, you're the winner—you'll have the weekend free. If you don't make it through your work, then you can skip the activities."

This proposal seemed reasonable to Jennifer, and that very evening she tackled the history book, using the Evelyn Wood approach to learning.

Each page of the book contained about 400 words, and 120 pages had been assigned. That meant Jennifer had to read approximately 48,000 words.

Using the basic Evelyn Wood method of layered or multiple-exposure reading, she first *overviewed* the book. That entailed looking at the cover and flap copy, the table of contents, the introduction and the conclusion. Also, she flipped through the book at a rate of about one to two seconds a page.

During the five minutes Jennifer spent in overviewing, she noted that in presenting George Washington's life, the author seemed interested in exploding or confirming myths and legends like the cutting down of the cherry tree.

In this short period, she obtained a good sense of the overall thrust or big picture of the book. Not only that, she came up with a host of questions about Washington she wanted answered—so she was well on her way to setting solid goals for her study.

Now, it was time for a closer look at the text—a *preview*. Jennifer knew that with a nonfiction textbook, it was usually best to preview, read and postview one chapter at a time. Also, a set of outlines or recall patterns should be built up chapter by chapter.

But in this case, because the book was relatively short and well-written, with an integrated narrative movement, she decided to preview the whole thing at once. Moving along at a rate of about four seconds per page, she began to identify large sections, boldface headings and major concepts.

This preview process took Jennifer about eight minutes, and she also devoted two minutes to drawing up a basic recall pattern, which contained the main headings in the book. The total time she had put in so far on the book was only fifteen minutes—and she was already well on her way toward learning what she needed for that Monday quiz.

Next, Jennifer began to *read*. At a pace averaging sixteen seconds per page, she read every word in the book and also filled in her notes with many details that she hadn't picked up during the overview and preview.

Unlike an untrained reader, she had the gestalt of the book in mind. In addition, she had a definite sense of where the author was taking her and a host of questions she wanted him to answer.

The background she had gained from the first two exposures to the book—or the first two layers of contact—now enabled her to move along easily at sixteen seconds per page and to finish the book in thirty-two minutes. How fast was she moving? She had read the text at her accustomed reading rate of 1,500 words per minute.

During her reading, she placed check marks lightly in the text to note key facts and concepts she wanted to include in her notes. Upon finishing the first reading, she decided to reread the book at a faster pace of about 3,000 words per minute and to focus on the checked passages. This rereading required sixteen minutes, and revising and adding to her recall pattern took about four.

Now, Jennifer was ready for the *postview* phase of study. With her recall patterns at hand, she went back through the book at a rate of about four seconds a page. During this eight-minute exercise, she checked to see how the various sections of the book related to one another. Also, she added a few additional points and details to fill out her notes.

When Jennifer finally sat back and surveyed her completed work on the book, even she was amazed at what she had accomplished.

In the first place, she saw that the total time she had devoted to this seemingly formidable history assignment was only one hour and fifteen minutes! Yet she had gone through the book five times (including two complete readings); generated many thoughts; answered scores of questions; and compiled an extremely useful set of notes for her test.

In reflecting on how much time this assignment *might* have taken, Jennifer recalled two approaches to study she had used in the past.

She might simply have plowed through this book at her usual subvocal linear reading rate of only about 400 words per minute. And that would have included no overview, no preview, and no note-taking. Then, she would have taken some extra time to go through the text again and make copious notes.

She knew from experience that no matter how she tried it, recording the notes after the reading would have been excruciating. She would have been required to reread the material at a slow subvocal linear rate (in her case, probably about 200 words per minute) as she jotted down the important facts and concepts.

Alternatively, she sometimes elected to jot some notes down during her first reading, but that approach also presented a host of problems. For one thing, she usually tried to develop a written outline without any idea of where the book was heading. Also, she was frequently in the dark about whether the facts and concepts she was recording had any particular significance. Of course, this kind of note-taking during the reading process would have slowed her reading down to a crawl—usually no more than about 100 words per minute.

How much time would Jennifer have spent using one of her old methods of study? Realistically, Jennifer had to admit that what she had accomplished in one hour and fifteen minutes with the Evelyn Wood approach would have taken at least six to eight hours with either of her old methods. That would have forced her to spend the rest of the evening and part or most of the next on the history book— just to get through it once and take some notes. She also knew that significant revision of the notes would have been required to prepare them as a study tool for the test.

As it was, she had finished with the basic assignment entirely in a little over one hour and could now move on to her other assignments—which she also planned to do using the Evelyn Wood learning strategies.

All that remained for Jennifer to accomplish before the history test the following Monday was to *review* her notes and perhaps glance through the text another time or two. During this final phase of her study, she planned to focus on those areas that she expected the teacher to emphasize on the test.

The review process took less than one leisurely hour, which she scheduled for a convenient time on the weekend. In fact, she could have spent even less time on the review than she did, but she wanted to be sure she really nailed the test.

Jennifer easily completed all her other assignments by Friday, and as a result, she was able to attend—and enjoy —her various weekend activities. And she did very well on her two quizzes and paper.

Like many other students who learn the techniques I'm describing in this book, Jennifer knew what was required to achieve Mental Soaring and, in fact, she was quite skilled at the process. But she hadn't gained the confidence she needed to actually apply those skills to a real-life situation.

As we continue with this discussion, try using the concepts I'm talking about on this book and on your other reading. It's only by doing what I'm talking about that you'll learn how these methods work in practice. Also, as you acquire experience, you'll automatically gain the self-assurance you need to engage in supersonic reading and studying.

So now, try putting into practice some of these principles that I've been preaching. Most likely, you haven't overviewed this book. Do so at this point, and then return to this section of the text.

———

Next, the following information on hand motions will enable you to incorporate still another prerequisite skill for layered study. These techniques are *absolutely fundamental* for developing maximum speed and efficiency in every step of learning that we've discussed—overviewing, previewing, reading, postviewing and reviewing.

## *ACTION DIGEST*

*1.* For the fastest reading speeds, you must observe the four basic principles of layered reading.

- See and accept words and phrases out of their normal order.
- Accept visual reassurance as you read.
- Read vertically.
- Understand the gestalt.

*2.* Know the five steps in layered reading, or the Multiple Reading Process: overview, preview, reading, postview, review.

# 5

# *How to Fly with Your Hands*

One of the major identifying marks of the Evelyn Wood approach to reading has been the use of hand motions. Upon seeing a person's hand or finger sweeping back and forth, up and down on a page in strange or exotic movements, a typical first response may be: "That's an Evelyn Wood student."

As you already know, Evelyn discovered the hand-motion concept as she was brushing dirt off a book that she had tossed down on the ground. In cleaning off each page, she began to read simultaneously at supersonic speeds—and thus the Wood hand-motion concept was born.

Over the years, this technique has been refined so that now there are many possible hand movements for every step of studying and reading. Also, when a student becomes adept at using several of the standard motions, he may want to experiment with his own personal variations. A number of our students have even formulated completely new techniques that are more appropriate to special tastes or needs.

Why use hand motions at all? They serve three basic functions:

- They help establish the fastest possible pace or rhythm for eye movements during the study of written material.
- They enhance concentration. Remember, if you're not paying attention to the words when you use this technique, you'll just be wiggling your hand on the page—and few people will allow themselves to do that for very long.
- They prevent regression, or going back over material you've already read.

Now let's consider how the major hand motions work. Many of the following explanations, beginning with the underlining motion which you've already learned, are accompanied by illustrative diagrams. The darkened path on each of these diagrams indicates the route your hand should follow in executing the motions.

## The Underlining Hand Motion

You've already learned this motion in chapter two, and I hope you're using it now as you read this part of the text.

To refresh your memory, here's an explanation of how the underlining motion works, with an illustrative diagram. Remember, this hand motion is most appropriate for the slower, subvocal linear reading.

How to execute the motion:

1. Place the palm of your hand on the page, with your thumb close to or tucked under the palm.

(*Note:* Throughout these explanations, assume that right-handed people will usually use their right hands, and left-handers, their left.)

2. Your fingers should be relaxed and spread slightly, with your hand relatively flat on the page.
3. The movement should be done smoothly, with the hand moving steadily across the page, under every line. Your eyes should keep pace with the hand.
4. At the end of each line, lift your fingers one-fourth to one-half inch above the page.
5. Bring your hand back diagonally down to the beginning of the next line, place your hand under it and repeat the underlining motion across the page.
6. Continue down the page.

## Diagram of the Underlining Hand Motion

XXXXXX XXXX XXXXX XXX XXXXX XXXXXXX XXXXX XXXXX
XXXXXXX XXXX XXX XXXX XXXXX XXXX XXX XXX XX XXXXXX
XXXX XXXXX XXXXXXXX XXX XX XXXXXX XXX XX XXXXXX XXX
XXXX XXXX XX XXXXXX XXX XX X XXXX XXXXX XXXX XXXXXXX
XXXX XXXX XXXXXX XXX XX XX XXXXX XX XXXX XXX XXX XXXX
XXX XXX XX XXX

XXXXXX XXXX XXXXX XXX XXXXX XXXXXXX XXXXX XXXXX
XXXXXXX XXXX XXX XXXX XXXXX XXXX XXX XXX XX XXXXXX
XXXX XXXXX XXXXXXXX XXX XX XXXXXX XXX XX XXXXXX XXX
XXXX XXXX XX XXXXXX XXX XX X XXXX XXXXX XXXX XXXXXXX
XXXX XXXX XXXXXX XXX XX XX XXXXX XX XXXX XXXX XXXX XX
XXXX XXX XXX XXXX XXX XXX XX XXX

XXXXXX XXXX XXXXX XXX XXXXX XXXXXXX XXXXX XXXXX
XXXXXXX XXXX XXX XXXX XXXXX XXXX XXX XXX XX XXXXXX
XXXX XXXXX XXXXXXXX XXX XX XXXXXX XXX XX XXXXXX XXX
XXXX XXXX XX XXXXXX XXX XX X XXXX XXXXX XXXX XXXXXXX
XXXX XXXX XXXXXX XXX XX XX XXXXX XX XXXX XXXX XXXX XX
XXXXXX XXX XX X XXXX XXX XXX XX XXX

XXXXXX XXXX XXXXX XXX XXXXX XXXXXXX XXXXX XXXXX
XXXXXXX XXXX XXX XXXX XXXXX XXXX XXX XXX XX XXXXXX
XXXX XXXXX XXXXXXXX XXX XX XXXXXX XXX XX XXXXXX XXX
XXXX XXXX XX XXXXXX XXX XX X XXXX XXXXX XXXX XXXXXXX
XXXX XXXX XXXXXX XXX XX XX XXXXX XX XXXX XXXX XXXX XX
XXXXXX XXX XX X XXXX XXX XXX XXXX XXX XXX

XXXXXX XXXX XXXXX XXX XXXXX XXXXXXX XXXXX XXXXX
XXXXXXX XXXX XXX XXXX XXXXX XXXX XXX XXX XX XXXXXX
XXXX XXXXX XXXXXXXX XXX XX XXXXXX XXX XX XXXXXX XXX
XXXX XXXX XX XXXXXX XXX XX X XXXX XXXXX XXXX XXXXXXX
XXXX XXXX XXXXXX XXX XX XX XXXXX XX XXXX XXXX XXXX XX
XXXXXX XXX XX X XXXX XXX XXX XXX XXX XX XXX

XXXXXX XXXX XXXXX XXX XXXXX XXXXXXX XXXXX XXXXX

## The S Hand Motion

This motion can be used in a number of ways. Some people like to use a broad, sweeping, "lazy" S motion during the previewing phase, when they're going through a book at a rate of about 2–4 seconds per page. Many people also use a tighter version of this movement when they're reading at supersonic speed.

How to execute the motion:

1. Place your palm on the page, with the thumb close to or tucked under the palm.
2. Your fingers should be relaxed and spread slightly, with the hand lying relatively flat on the page.
3. Begin the movement two lines from the top of the page. (Again, right-handers should use their right hand, left-handers their left.) Sweep your hand from the left to the right; move your hand down about three lines on the right side of the page; and return the hand horizontally across to the left side of the page.
4. Repeat the motion several times down the page and then begin again on the next page.
5. Your eyes need not follow the tips of your fingers while you read, as they do with the underlining motion. But they should move down the page at the same pace as the hand. A major goal with this motion is to try to see as many words as possible with one look, rather than focusing on single words.

Note that the S motion is a reverse S, since you begin it on the opposite side of the page from where a proper S would start.

The following diagram illustrates a relatively tight S motion, more appropriate for reading than previewing. But this is a flexible motion which you can adjust to fit the preview or other purposes.

## Diagram of the S Hand Motion

XXXXXX XXXX XXXXX XXX XXXXX XXXXXXX XXXXX XXXXX
XXXXXXX XXXX XXX XXXX XXXX XXXX XXX XXX XX XXXXXX
XXXX XXXXX XXXXXXXX XXX XX XXXXXX XXX XX XXXXXX XX
XXXX XXXX XX XXXXXX XXX XX X XXXX XXXXX XXXX XXXXXX
XXX XXXX XXXXXX XXX XX XX XXXX XX XXXX XXX XXX XXXX
XXX XXX XX XXX

XXXXXX XXXX XXXX XXX XXXXX XXXXXX XXXXX XXXXX
XXXXXXX XXXX XXX XXXX XXXXX XXXX XXX XXX XX XX XXXX
XXXX XXXXX XXXXXXXX XXX XX XXXXXX XXX XX XXXXX XXX
XXXX XXXX XX XXXXXX XXX XX X XXXX XXXXX XXXX XXXXXXX
XXXX XXXX XXXXXX XXX XX XX XXXXX XX XXXX XXXX XXXX XX
XXXX XXX XXX XXXX XXX XXX XX XXX

XXXXXX XXXX XXXXX XXX XXXXX XXXXXX XXXXX XXXXX
XXXXXXX XXXX XXX XXXX XXXXX XXXX XXX XXX XX XX XXXX
XXXX XXXXX XXXXXXXX XXX XX XXXXXX XXX XX XXXXXX XX
XXXX XXXX XX XXXXXX XXX XX X XXXX XXXXX XXXX XXXXXX
XXX XXXX XXXXXX XXX XX XX XXXXX XX XXXX XXXX XXXX XX
XXX XXX XXX XX X XXXX XXX XXX XX XXX

XXXXXX XXXX XXXXX XXX XXXXX XXXXXX XXXXX XXXXX
XXXXXXX XXXX XXX XXXX XXXXX XXXX XXX XXX XX XXXX X
XXXX XXXXX XXXXXXXX XXX XX XXXXXX XXX XX XXXXXX XX
XXXX XXXX XX XXXXXX XXX XX XX X XXXX XXXXX XXXX XXXX
XXX XXXX XXXXXX XXX XX XX XXXXX XX XXXX XXXX XXXX XX
XXXX XXX XX X XXXX XXX XXX XXXX XXX XXX

XXXXXX XXXX XXXXX XXX XXXXX XXXXXXX XXXX XXXXX
XXXXXXX XXXX XXX XXXX XXXXX XXXX XXX XXX XX XX XXXX
XXXX XXXXX XXXXXXXX XXX XX XXXXXX XXX XX XXXXXX XX
XXXX XXXX XX XXXXXX XXX XX X XXXX XXXXX XXXX XXXXXXX
XXX XXXX XXXXXX XXX XX XX XXXXX XX XXXX XXXX XXXX XX
XXXXX XXX XX X XXXX XXX XXX XXXX XXX XXX XX XXX

XXXXXX XXXX XXXXX XXX XXXXX XXXXXXX XXXXX XXXXX

## *The Question Mark*

This motion, which looks like a question mark, can be used for a fast review of material during the preview or even the overview stage. This movement can easily be executed at a rate of 2–4 seconds per page. With practice, it can be completed at a rate of one second a page.

*Caution:* When some people begin to move their hands faster on a page, they may irritate or even blister the tips of their fingers. You can avoid this discomfort by keeping *very* light contact with the page or executing the motion above the page when you move at very high speeds.

How to execute the motion:

1. Place your palm on the page, with your thumb close to or tucked under the palm.
2. Your fingers should be relaxed and spread slightly, with the hand relatively flat on the page.
3. Begin the movement a line or two from the top of the upper left-hand side of the page. Proceed to sweep across the entire page with one large question-mark-shaped hand motion. Your hand movement should end at the center of the bottom of the page.
4. Again, don't worry about trying to lock your eyes on the precise route you trace with your fingers. Remember, a major purpose of hand motions is simply to keep your eyes moving on the page, regardless of where your hand is.
5. Repeat with subsequent pages.

## Diagram of the Question-Mark Hand Motion

XXXXXX XXXX XXXXX XXX XXXXX XXXXXXX XXXXX XXXXX
XXXXXXX XXXX XXX XXXX XXXXX XXXX XXX XXX XX XXXXXX
XXXX XXXXX XXXXXXXX XXX XX XXXXXX XXX XX XXXXXX XXX
XXXX XXXX XX XXXXXX XXX XX X XXXX XXXXX XXXX XXXXXX
XXXX XXXX XXXXXX XXX XX XX XXXXX XX XXXX XXX XXX XXXX
XXX XXX XX XXX

XXXXXX XXXX XXXXX XXX XXXXX XXXXXXX XXXXX XXXXX
XXXXXXX XXXX XXX XXXX XXXXX XXXX XXX XXX XX XX XXXX
XXXX XXXXX XXXXXXXX XXX XX XXXXXX XXX XX XXXXX XXX
XXXX XXXX XX XXXXXX XXX XX X XXXX XXXXX XXXX XXXXXX
XXXX XXXX XXXXXX XXX XX XX XXXXX XX XXXX XXXX XXXX XX
XXXX XXX XXX XXXX XXX XXX XX XXX

XXXXXX XXXX XXXXX XXX XXXXX XXXXXXX XXXXX XXXXX
XXXXXXX XXXX XXX XXXX XXXXX XXXX XXX XXX XX XXXXXX
XXXX XXXXX XXXXXXXX XXX XX XXXXX XXX XX XXXXXX XXX
XXXX XXXX XX XXXXXX XXX XX X XXXX XXXX XXXX XXXXXXX
XXXX XXXX XXXXXX XXX XX XX XXXX XX XXXX XXXX XXXX XX
XXXXXX XXX XX X XXXX XXX XXX XX XXX

XXXXXX XXXX XXXXX XXX XXXXX XXXXXXX XXXXX XXXXX
XXXXXXX XXXX XXX XXXX XXXX XXXX XXX XXX XX XXXXXX
XXXX XXXXX XXXXXXXX XXX XX XXXXXX XXX XX XXXXXX XXX
XXXX XXXX XX XXXXXX XXX XX X XXXX XXXXX XXXX XXXXXXX
XXXX XXXX XXXXXX XXX XX XX XXXXX XX XXXX XXXX XXXX XX
XXXXXX XXX XX X XXXX XXX XXX XXXX XXX XXX

XXXXXX XXXX XXXXX XXX XXXXX XXXXXXX XXXXX XXXXX
XXXXXXX XXXX XXX XXXX XXXXX XXXX XXX XXX XX XXXXXX
XXXX XXXXX XXXXXXXX XXX XX XXXXXX XXX XX XXXXXX XXX
XXXX XXXX XX XXXXXX XXX XX X XXXX XXXXX XXXX XXXXXXX
XXXX XXXX XXXXXX XXX XX XX XXXXX XX XXXX XXXX XXXX XX
XXXXXX XXX XX X XXXX XXX XXX XXXX XXX XXX XX XXX

XXXXXX XXXX XXXXX XXX XXXXX XXXXXXX XXXXX XXXXX

## *The X Hand Motion*

This angular movement is especially useful when you're reading newspapers, magazines, journal articles or other material that's printed in columns.

Because the **X** motion is a little harder to coordinate than ones already described, you'll probably have to practice this one several times before it feels natural.

How to execute the motion:

1. Don't linger over any word or line with this motion— execute it quickly.
2. Start at the top left corner of the page. Move your index finger diagonally down and across the page to the right until your hand reaches the right-hand side of the page, about five lines from the top.
3. Without stopping, switch to your middle finger and move it up with a sharp-cornered, angular movement to the second line from the top of the page, along the right-hand edge of the print.
4. Then immediately corner sharply again and angle your middle finger diagonally across the page to the left until you reach the left-hand margin. Your target should be a point several lines below the line at which you stopped on the right-hand margin.
5. Now, shift back to your index finger and move it up sharply about three lines along the left-hand edge of print.
6. Finally, move down and across the page diagonally with your forefinger, as you did in Step 1.
7. Repeat these movements down the page.

## Diagram of the X Hand Motion

XXXXXX XXXX XXXXX XXX XXXXX XXXXXXX XXXXX XXXXX
XXXXXXX XXXX XXX XXXX XXXXX XXXX XXX XXX XX XXXXXX
XXXX XXXXX XXXXXXXX XXX XX XXXXXXX XXX XX XXXXXX XXX
XXXX XXXX XX XXXXXX XXX XX X XXXX XXXXX XXXX XXXXXXX
XXXX XXXX XXXXXX XXX XX XX XXXXXX XX XXXX XXX XXX XXXX
XXX XXX XX XXX

XXXXXX XXXX XXXXX XXX XXXXX XXXXXXX XXXXX XXXXX
XXXXXXX XXXX XXX XXXX XXXXX XXXX XXXXXX XX XXXXXX
XXXX XXXXX XXXXXXX XXX XX XXXXXX XXX XX XX XXXXXX XXX
XXXX XXXX XX XXXXXX XXX XX X XXXX XXXXX XXXX XXXXXXX
XXXX XXXX XXXXXX XXX XX XX XXXXXX XX XXXX XXXX XXXX XX
XXXX XXX XXX XXXX XXX XXX XX XXX

XXXXXX XXXX XXXXX XXX XXXXX XXXXXXX XXXXX XXXXX
XXXXXX XXXX XXX XXXX XXXX XXXX XXX XXX XX XXXXXX
XXXX XXXXX XX XXXXXX XXX XX XXXXXX XXX XX XXXXXX XXX
XXXX XXXX XX XX XXXXXX XX XXXX XXXXX XXXX XXXXXXX
XXXXX XXX XX X XXXX XXX XXX XX XXX

XXXXXX XXXX XXXXX XXX XXX XXXXXXX XXXXX XXXXX
XXXXXXX XXXX XXX XXXX XXXXX XXX XXX XXX XX XXXXXX
XXXX XXXXXX XX XXXXXX XXX XX XXXXXXX XXX XX XXXXXX XXX
XXXX XXXX XX XXXXXX XXX XX XX XXXXXX XX XXXX XXXX XX
XXXXX XXX XX X XXXX XXX XXX XX XXX

XXXXXX XXXX XXXXX XXX XXXXX XXXXXXX XXXXX XXXXX
XXXXXXX XXXX XXX XXXX XXXXX XXXX XXX XXX XX XXXXXX
XXXX XXXX XXXXXXXX XXX XX XX XXXXXX XXX XXXXXXX XX
XXXX XXXX XX XXXXXX XXX XXX XXX XXXXX XXXX XXXXXXX
XXXX XXXX XXXXXX XXX XX XX XXXX XX XXXX XXXX XXXX XX
XXXXX XXX XX X XXXX XXX XXX XXX XXX

XXXXXX XXXX XXXXX XXX XXXXX XXXXXX XXXXX XXXXX
XXXXXXX XXXX XXX XXXX XXXXX XXXX XXX XXX XX XXXX
XXXX XXXXX XXXXXXXXX XX XX XXXXXX XXX XX XXXXXX XXX
XXXX XXXX XXXXXX XXX XX XX XXXX XX XXXX XXXXX XX
XXXXXX XXX XX X XXXX XXX XXX XXXX XXX

XXXXXX XXXX XXXXX XXX XXXXX XXXXXXX XXXXX XXXXX

98

## *The Loop Hand Motion*

This movement, like the X motion, can be used for materials like newspapers or journal articles that are printed in columns. But unlike the X, the loop involves tracing curved, rather than angular turns on the page.

Some people prefer this motion for reading and previewing assignments on book-size pages.

How to execute the motion:

1. Begin with the index or middle finger at the upper left-hand corner of the page. Sweep this finger down three to five lines and across the page diagonally to the right margin.
2. Next, move the finger up in a slightly curving motion two or three lines along the right margin.
3. Then execute a sharp curve and guide your finger down four to six lines across the page until you reach the left margin.
4. Finally, trace a slight curved line two or three lines up the left-hand margin.
5. Then execute another sharp curve and move the finger down diagonally across the page as you did in Step 1.
6. Repeat this pattern until you've finished the page.

## Diagram of the Loop Hand Motion

## *The L Hand Motion*

As with the **X** and loop techniques, this movement is quite useful in reading material printed in columns, but it can also be used for other types of previewing and reading.

In some respects, the physical shape of this motion is a combination of the underlining, the **X** and the loop.

How to execute the motion:

1. Using your index finger, begin two lines down from the top of the page on the left-hand side.
2. Move the index finger from the left to the right of the page under the line.
3. When you reach a point about a half-inch from the right-hand margin, move the finger up the page two lines in a slow curve.
4. Then sweep your finger down across the page about five or six lines to the left margin.
5. Now, move the finger upward two lines in a slow curve. Then, begin to trace that finger under the line of type in an underlining pattern, as you did in Step 2.
6. Repeat down the page.

## Diagram of the L Hand Motion

XXXXXX XXXX XXXXX XXX XXXXX XXXXXXX XXXXX XXXX XXX
XXXXXX XXXX XXX XXXX XXXXX XXX XX XXXXXXX
XXXX XXXXX XXXXXXX XXX XX XXXX XXX XX XXXXXX XXX
XXXX XXXX XX XXXXXX XXX XX X XXXX XXXXX XXXX XXXXXX
XX XXX XX XXX
XXXXXX XXXX XXXXX XX XXXXX XXXXXXX XXX XXXX
XXXXXXX XXXX XXX XXXXX XXX XXXX XXX XX XX XX XX
XXX XXXXX XX XXXXXX XXX X XXXX XXXXX XXX
XXXX XXXX XXXXXX XX XX XXXXX XX XXX XXXX XXXX
XXXXX XXXX XXXXX XX XXXXX XXXXXXX XXXX
XXXXXXX XXXX XXX XXX XXXXX XXXX XXX XX XXXXX
XXX XXXXX XX XXXX XXX XX XXXXXX XXX
XXX XXXX XXXXXX XX XX XXXXX XX XXXX XXX XXXX
XXXXXX XXX XX XXXXXX XXX XX XXXXX XXXX XXXX
XXXXXXX XXXX XXX XXX XXXXX XXXX XXX XX XXXXX
XXX XXXXX XX XXXXXX XXX XX XX XXXXXX XXX
XXXX XXXX XXXXXX XX XX XX XXXXX XX XXXX XXXX XXX
XXXX XXXXX XXX XXX XXXXXXX XXXXX XXXXX
XXXXXXX XXXX XXX XXXX XXXX XXXX XXX XXX XXXXX
XXX XXXXX XX XXXXXX XXX XX X XXXX XXXXX XXXX XXXXXXX
XXXX XXXX XXXXXX XXX XX X XXXX XX XXXX XXXX XXXX XX
XXXXXX XXXX XXXXX XXX XXXXX XXXXXXX XXXXX XXXXX

## *Other Ways to Fly with Your Hands*

These six motions represent the basic ways to use hand motions to pace your reading. But there are also many others that you may find useful. Here are some of the possibilities:

**The horseshoe.** Many of our top readers have found a horseshoe-shaped motion to be particularly helpful for the extremely fast overviewing phases of study. Acquiring its name from the horseshoe-shaped pattern that the hand traces, this movement works like this:

1. Using your *left* hand as a pacer, you begin with the left hand at the top of the *right*-hand page. Your right hand should be poised at the upper right-hand corner of the right page, ready to turn the page when appropriate.
2. Sweep your left hand straight down the right page.
3. Move the left hand across the bottom of the book in a curved motion until it reaches the bottom of the left-hand page.
4. Then, sweep the left hand straight up to the top of the left page.
5. When your left hand reaches the top of the left page, immediately flip the right page over with your right hand. Move your left hand to the top of the next right-hand page, and repeat the movement with the next set of pages.
6. Your eyes should move over the two pages at the same pace that your left hand is moving, though the eyes need not follow precisely in the path of the hand.

As you can see, this movement requires you to look through the book out of the normal order in which it's written. Yet you can expect to understand much of what you see, even though you take it in out of the usual word sequence. Remember: Your brain is structured so that you're not limited in your intake of information by the way words and ideas are presented on a page.

Note that this movement should only take about one to two seconds to complete for each set of two pages. So you shouldn't expect to see or read every word, or even to understand most of what you do see.

Remember, this is an overviewing hand motion, so you're supposed to move very fast and simply take in a few key concepts and the basic structure of the book. Later previewing and reading will provide more opportunity for absorbing details.

**The U hand motion.** A variation on the horseshoe movement is the U, which is executed in the reverse direction across the book. This motion can be used for overviewing or previewing.

1. Begin with the *right* hand at the top of the *left*-hand page. The left arm and hand cradle the book in a standard page-turning position. The left hand, poised to turn the page, holds the upper right-hand edge of the right page.
2. Then sweep the right hand, palm downward, straight down the left-hand page.
3. When you reach the bottom of that page, move the right hand over to the bottom to the right-hand page.
4. Sweep it straight upward to the top of the page. (Some prefer to execute this move with the right hand turned palm upward.)

5. When you reach the top of the right-hand page, turn the page with the left hand.
6. Repeat the same pattern with the following pages.

**The brush.** When Evelyn Wood first formulated the brush hand motion, she was cleaning dirt off *Green Mansions,* which she had tossed on the ground.

The average student may find the brush stroke most helpful when he's under considerable pressure or subject to distractions. For example, this technique may be used for reading exam questions or for reading when there's a lot of noise in the study area, as often happens in dormitory rooms.

In most cases, students in distracting environments should leave and find a quieter place, more conducive to concentration. But sometimes, it's not possible to find a better site for study, especially if you have only a short time to go over material. In these situations, the brush stroke can work quite well.

1. Using the back of your right hand at the top of the left-hand page, begin brushing your hand across the page, moving it steadily downward.
2. When you've finished the left page, move your hand immediately to the top of the right-hand page, and repeat.
3. Then turn the page in the standard way with the left hand.

**The half-moon.** This is another motion that some people like to use during the reading phase of study.

To execute it, follow these steps:

1. Begin with the left hand or one finger, palm down on the upper left-hand portion of the left page.

2. Move the hand in a shallow, half-moon-shaped curve downward and across the page and then upward to the upper right-hand section of the left page.
3. Then, using the same curved, scooping motion, move the hand back again to the left margin, but this time across a lower portion of the text.
4. Continue back and forth until you've finished the left page, and then repeat with the right page.

There are many other motions that skilled readers have found to be useful. In fact, the possibilities are almost limitless and depend primarily on what works best for the individual student.

For example, a number of students have developed a variation on what they call the crawl. This involves moving the fingers of the right hand in a crawling motion down each page, from top to bottom.

Other students make a fist with their right hand and then extend their right forefinger and little finger in a horn configuration. As they move their hands down the page, their eyes move around between the extended fingers.

You should feel free to experiment with these and other hand motions as you develop your expertise in reading. For now, however, I'd suggest you stick with the standard hand motion techniques I've described.

Now, let's try using some of these hand motions.

First, practice overviewing with the horseshoe motion. Since you've already overviewed the book once, just go over the next chapter at the rate of about a second a page with the horseshoe. Then return to this point in the text.

Now try previewing the next chapter with the question-mark motion. You should move along at a pace of about four seconds a page. When you've finished, return to this point once again.

Finally, read the next chapter using a relatively tight S motion. Although you should move through it at a comfortable rate that allows you to see every word, try to read at a pace of no more than fifteen seconds per page. If you feel you've missed too much after finishing the chapter at this speed, feel free to reread it. You'll have plenty of time because at fifteen seconds per page, you'll have been reading at a rate in excess of 1,000 words per minute!

## *ACTION DIGEST*

**1.** Hand motions help you read faster, enhance concentration and discourage regression.

**2.** Some possible hand motions include underlining, the S, the question mark, the X, the L, the loop, the horseshoe, the U, the brush, and the half-moon.

# 6

# *Preparing Your Own "Mental Computer Printout"*

What's the main goal of reading and studying school assignments?

That's an easy question: Most students want to be able to remember and use the material they go through so that they can do well on tests and papers.

And what's the best way to enable yourself to remember and use these materials?

Again, an easy answer: Take notes.

But most people don't know how to take notes that really help them remember and use important facts and concepts on tests and in papers. Average students tend to take notes on books and articles in one of two ways. They write copiously in prose essay style, line after line in a notebook, with few or any paragraphs. Or they write copiously in an outline format, with various items indented under other items; but often there's little forethought or planning.

Unfortunately, these approaches are both counterproductive because they encourage the brain to stay out of the process of learning and remembering. Such heavy, basically unorganized note-taking employs the eyes and the hands much more than the mind.

With these two methods, the student mainly sees the material on the page, and then, without thinking much about it, records what he has just seen on a piece of paper. There's little or no critical evaluation and no attempt to fix the main points in the memory.

In contrast, there are other techniques that will engage your mind at an early stage in studying. In effect, it's possible to turn your brain into a space-age computer, and transform your note-taking into a kind of "mental computer printout" that reflects a personal and profound understanding of the material. The end result should be a significant enhancement of your ability to remember and use the material you study.

## What's a Recall Pattern?

At the Evelyn Wood program, we prefer to call our lesson notes "recall patterns," because their main function is to enable you to organize and then draw easily and efficiently on the material you've taken in during study sessions.

The ability to recall is the ability to write or relate orally, in your own words, information that you've gained from what you've read. By this definition, then, recalling is directly tied into the process of remembering.

The student who has a good memory, along with an ability to make an intelligent presentation of the facts and concepts remembered, is going to earn the highest grades. In fact, you might say that the achievements of all honors students begin with the art of committing key information to memory.

Two of the main elements that promote a good memory are strong associations between different items of information and powerful impressions made on the mind by the assigned material. Many memory experts recommend, for example, that you link different items together through mental pictures. Also, they may suggest that you root them in dramatic, absurd or amusing thoughts or emotions.

Suppose you want to remember a group of unconnected items on a shopping list. These might include catsup, lettuce, carrots, celery, toilet paper, beets, oranges and toothpaste. Remembering these eight items without writing them down may be chancy, especially if you have a lot of other things on your mind. But if you link them together into an absurd picture in your mind, remembering becomes much easier.

For example, you might picture these items as part of a funny little "grocery man": His body is the catsup bottle; his head is the lettuce; one arm is a carrot; another arm is a piece of celery; his eyes are beets; his nose is an orange; he's on a street lined with toilet paper; and he's riding a toothpaste-tube-shaped rocket ship. If you know there are ten items and you associate them in this absurd but connected sequence, you're much more likely to remember all of them.

The same principles apply when you're taking notes. There's very little that's memorable about writing sentence after sentence in a notebook. But if you structure your notes into a logically connected, visually impressive pattern on the paper, you're much more likely to recall later what you've written.

## *A New Way of Taking Notes*

**A personal "mental printout."** A recall pattern has a completely different look from ordinary study notes. In a sense, you might think of recall patterns as being analogous to computer spreadsheets or graphic representations of information. These patterns will allow your mind to generate memorable, highly useful images that are impossible with old-fashioned note-taking.

To illustrate what I mean, I'd like you to consider how some of our students have formulated recall patterns based on written material they were given on the very subject we're now discussing—recall patterns. The written material included a number of items we've already discussed as well as some other points. Here's a sampling of the raw material we supplied:

- A recall pattern is a picture of the written material.
- It makes use of lines, with main and subordinate ideas written on various branches.
- The pattern enables the student to design his own organization of study materials.
- Many students like to use pens or pencils of different colors in drawing a useful, memorable pattern. For example, a pencil may be best for tentative drawings during the overview or preview phase of study; a black pen can then be used for recalls finalized during previewing. Next, you may prefer to switch to red for additions made during reading; blue might be employed in the postview phase.
- The pattern is a method of taking notes quickly and helps encourage greater creativity and the generation of thoughts.

- The pattern should usually be drawn up and filled in while the book is *closed*. Obviously, the more you know about a subject, the more you can do patterns with the book closed. The more technical or unfamiliar the material, the less you should use the closed-book approach.
- Some major advantages of a recall pattern: It helps condense material; makes it easier to highlight associations between concepts; and provides an overall organization for what's been read.
- A recall pattern can be used in a variety of ways with different types of material. The possibilities include preserving material that's been read; remembering facts and ideas from reading, lectures or other meetings; planning your schedule; and otherwise documenting important information.

Now, here's a typical "slash" recall, which was drawn to record the above information on recall patterns.

## Sample Slash Recall Pattern

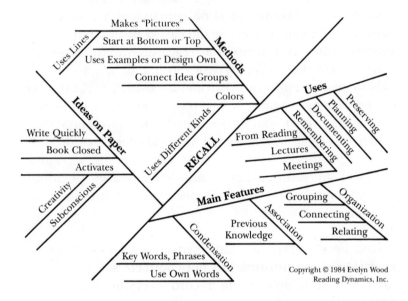

Copyright © 1984 Evelyn Wood
Reading Dynamics, Inc.

Many students initially find the innovative Evelyn Wood techniques for note-taking—like the slash recall—somewhat awkward or formidable. But as you'll see, a recall pattern is really the best way to take notes. Granted, it's necessary to master a few simple techniques for drawing these patterns. With just a little practice, however, this form of note-taking will become easier, *and* more efficient and useful, than your old way of operating.

**Drawing a recall pattern.** A recall pattern may first be formulated immediately after the overview. But often, especially with difficult nonfiction texts, the student will wait

114

until after the first preview of a book, chapter, or article to take notes. Here are some pointers.

After you've completed a preview, draw or create the basic structure and record initial entry of topics on a recall pattern in pencil. This way, you can erase preliminary information that later turns out to be inappropriate or incorrect.

Many students find that it's best to include a recall pattern for both the introduction and conclusion in each chapter. This can be done on a separate sheet of paper, or may be treated as one branch of the entire chapter's recall pattern.

Try to use subheadings, boldface items and other highlighted segments of texts as a guide. Many times, the subheadings in a chapter will become the main branches of the recall pattern.

In general, keep your recall pattern entries short. Use keys words and phrases, but not complete sentences. You can't and shouldn't try to record everything you read. Rather, draft notes that will stimulate your growing memory of the subject.

Read the chapter. After reading, put the book aside and insert more supporting facts and concepts. If you can't remember a point, feel free to pick the book up and reread that uncertain section. But again, don't just copy what's in the book onto your recall pattern. Being able to transfer information into your notes without being glued to the text is an important part of the learning process.

Do not slow down your overviewing, previewing or reading just because you're drafting a recall. Move along at your fastest possible pace when you're going through the book or article. Then put it aside and again, as quickly as possible, make your recall pattern entries.

The overviewing-previewing-reading and the recall or note-taking are separate, but they are also part of the entire time you devote to study. You can deal with all these activities much more efficiently if you treat them as individual entities.

If you started your recall pattern during the overview, begin to finalize the general structure after the preview. This is the time to fill in some of the main ideas in your pattern, preferably in a contrasting color. The more vividly you picture the material on paper—and the more memorable you can make the linkage between concepts—the more likely you are to remember it later.

Again, when you jot down information at this stage, it's important to write from memory—don't just copy material from the book.

Continue to revise and add to your recall pattern during the final postview and review phases of study. In fact, you may decide during these stages that you want to redraw your recall pattern completely. That's perfectly acceptable because the more you work with the material—the more you get into it—the more likely you'll be to understand and remember what you've read.

**What kind of pattern?** The most useful recall patterns usually fall into one of five basic categories: slash, linear, radial, pictorial and random.

First, look at the following models and the comments on the first four of these patterns (excluding, for the moment, the random pattern). Then, we'll examine each of these types in more detail, and you can decide which one best fits your needs.

## Model Slash and Linear Recall Patterns

| RECALL STYLE: | SAMPLE: | SUITABLE FOR: |
|---|---|---|

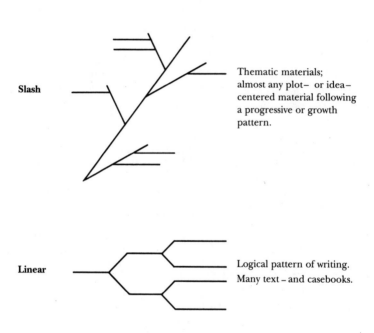

**Slash** — Thematic materials; almost any plot– or idea–centered material following a progressive or growth pattern.

**Linear** — Logical pattern of writing. Many text – and casebooks.

# Model Radial Recall Patterns

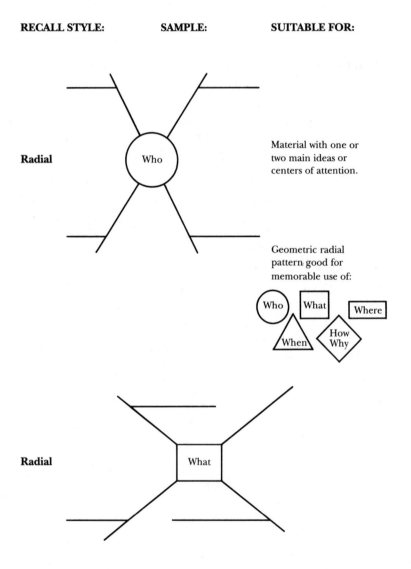

| RECALL STYLE: | SAMPLE: | SUITABLE FOR: |
|---|---|---|

**Radial** — Material with one or two main ideas or centers of attention.

Geometric radial pattern good for memorable use of:

**Radial**

## Model Pictorial Recall Patterns

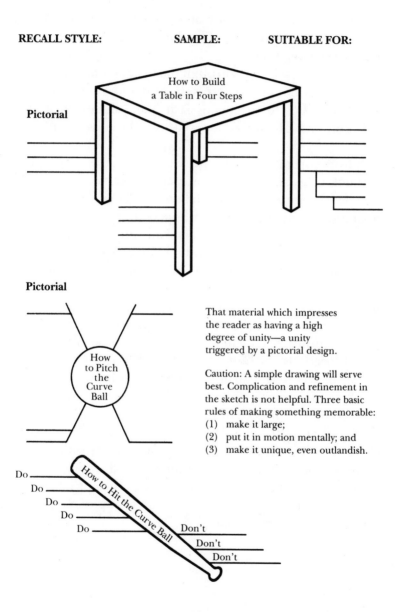

**RECALL STYLE:**    **SAMPLE:**    **SUITABLE FOR:**

**Pictorial**

How to Build
a Table in Four Steps

**Pictorial**

How
to Pitch
the
Curve
Ball

That material which impresses
the reader as having a high
degree of unity—a unity
triggered by a pictorial design.

Caution: A simple drawing will serve
best. Complication and refinement in
the sketch is not helpful. Three basic
rules of making something memorable:
(1)  make it large;
(2)  put it in motion mentally; and
(3)  make it unique, even outlandish.

How to Hit the Curve Ball

Do
Do
Do
Do
Do
Don't
Don't
Don't

**More on the slash.** The slash structure is perhaps the most popular and useful of all the recall patterns. You draw the basic slash line diagonally, beginning at the bottom of the left-hand corner of your note paper and ending at the upper right-hand corner. This line represents the major topic of your reading.

Then, after each time through the assigned material, you should make changes, if necessary, and add more branches or sub-branches to the main slash line. Subheadings and boldfaced or highlighted materials may be placed on these lines.

With important nonfiction textbooks, one page in your notebook is usually enough for each chapter. On the other hand, less important nonfiction books and many novels may only require one page for the whole text.

As I mentioned earlier, a major advantage of the slash, and of other recall patterns, is that you can see at a glance your notes on all the material covered in a given segment of reading. The material will automatically be organized logically: Subheadings will branch off the main topic and sub-subheadings will shoot off those branches.

If the author has included material on one subtopic in several locations in the text, your slash recall pattern will enable you to insert it all under one of your branches. You'll thus have it available for review in one spot, rather than spread out over piles of disorganized notes.

To give you an idea of how easily organization can be achieved with a slash recall, look at how it works with a long, assorted shopping list. If every complicated list were organized this way, think how much more efficient shopping would be. Using this approach, you can group related items together for ease in shopping.

# How a Slash Recall Can Organize a Shopping List

Apples
Dry Cereal
Sugar
Pork Chops
Milk
Eggs
Toilet Paper
Glass Cleaner
Bread
Rice
Peas
Broccoli
Chicken
Macaroni
Cheese
Potatoes
Green Beans
Lettuce
Tomatoes
Soft Drinks
Cucumbers
Ice Cream
Carrots
Shrimp
Sour Cream
Flour
Coffee
Paper Towels
Spareribs
Spinach
Hamburger
Bacon
Jam
Cheesecake
Beer
Paper Napkins
Cupcakes
Tuna
Cottage Cheese
Bananas
Steel Wool
Laundry Soap
Peaches

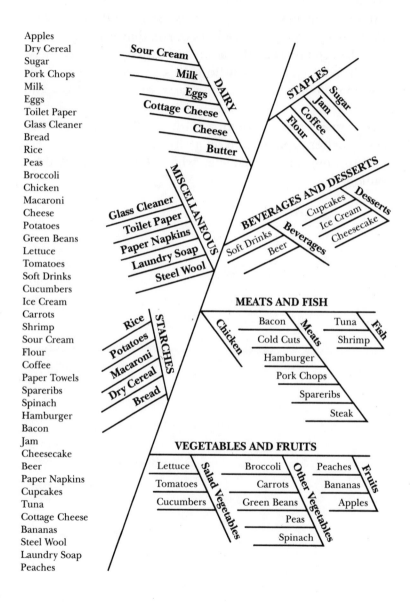

Here's another slash recall pattern, which has been a particularly helpful model for law students to use when they're taking notes on their cases.

Many of the best law students like to fit all their notes on a case on a single page. And of course, they want the material to be organized as efficiently as possible. Unfortunately, though, not every judge who writes an opinion is well organized or logical in presenting facts, principles of law and other points.

To remedy this problem, a slash recall pattern can help impose better organization on a difficult case than just writing down notes in the order in which the judge drafted his opinion.

# Model Slash Recall Pattern for Legal Cases

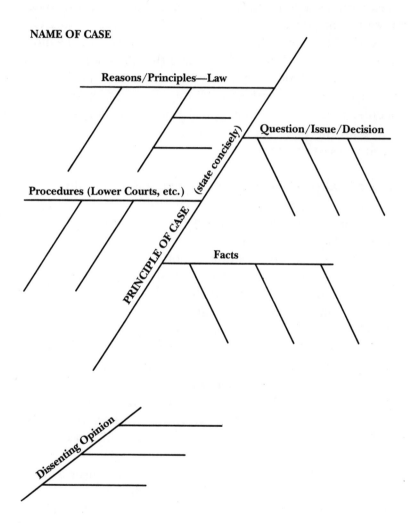

**The linear pattern.** This type resembles a traditional outline configuration more closely than any of the other recall patterns. Consequently, it's most useful when a text is very well organized or logical. Well-written scientific texts or lawbooks may lend themselves particularly well to this type of note-taking.

A number of people have found this approach to be most comfortable and familiar in making the transition from ordinary note-taking. But it may be harder to accommodate this pattern to complex or disorganized reading assignments. Also, students may find that it's harder to use all the space on the page with the linear method than with some of the more flexible patterns.

**The radial pattern.** This type of note-taking usually works best with material that has one or two main focuses. The branches that radiate out from the center can be used to describe or explain the main theme.

Students who are reading fiction often prefer this approach. For example, only one radial pattern may be used for short stories or relatively simple novels. The title might be placed in the center area, and then the main elements of the story—such as plot, characters and setting—can be entered on the main and subordinate branches.

With fiction that needs more extensive recalling, such as a massive novel like *War and Peace,* a separate radial pattern might be used for each of the main elements of the story. So you might have one pattern with characters as its organizing principle, another pattern for plot and still another one for setting.

The radial pattern also works well for journalistic articles that answer the five key questions, "Who? What? When? Where? How or why?" Again, one pattern might be used with the key questions indicated on the branches. Or a separate pattern can be employed for each of the main topics.

**The pictorial pattern.** Visually oriented people often have a lot of fun taking notes pictorially because the main idea is to draw a picture that represents the pertinent subject matter.

As you can see from the accompanying samples, a table might be used for a book or article called "How to Build a Table in Four Steps." Or a baseball bat may be appropriate for material that deals with hitting techniques.

A major advantage of pictorial patterns is that they are often very memorable. Try using this approach in your next note-taking effort, and see if the concepts aren't fixed more firmly in your mind after you put your books and notes away.

On the other hand, some people find it hard to come up with a good picture, and they seem to spend more time agonizing over their drawing than they do on the underlying subject matter. There may also be a tendency to make the picture too complicated—and complexity in this type of recall pattern will make note-taking much harder to do or remember.

In addition, you may come across important items in your reading that don't relate to the picture you've chosen. For example, suppose you're reading a book on Freudian psychology, and so you draw a picture of a person's head as your main note-taking focus.

But then the author shifts to a discussion of another psychological school. In that case, you might have to draw another pictorial recall pattern. Or it might have been advisable to use just one slash recall pattern for the entire reading assignment.

**The random pattern.** I've omitted a diagram of this approach because it's hard to include one general model or sample that's applicable in most situations. The main idea here is both to jot down facts, ideas and concepts at random, and to try to group them as you write in a way that imposes some sort of order on the whole.

In other words, suppose you're trying to draft a master recall pattern for an entire American literature course. In such a case, you might put Hawthorne in one corner of the paper, Poe in another corner, Hemingway in another part and so on.

Then, when you've recorded all your main topics, you might try relating them to one another with explanatory connecting lines. Or you might doodle for a while on this initial random pattern and eventually finalize your thoughts in a second draft.

The random pattern works best with extremely disorganized material or in situations where the student is trying to impose a single set of themes that weren't present or were unclear in the original notes. It may be just the tool to use when you need to impose order and relate disparate topics that have been covered in a course.

---

These are some of the most popular and efficient recall patterns that we've discovered in our research. But you may want to try something more creative. For example, you might use a combination of two or more of these patterns on a given assignment. Or you may even come up with completely different approaches that work better for your special needs.

If you're just beginning with the recall pattern concept, however, I'd suggest that you try the slash recall pattern first. To get some practice with this type of note-taking, preview the next chapter. Then close the book and draw a slash recall. Finally, read the chapter and add new information, as appropriate, to your original recall pattern.

## *ACTION DIGEST*

---

*1.* A recall pattern is the most effective and memorable way to take notes.

*2.* Possible recall patterns include the slash, linear, radial, pictorial and random.

---

# 7

# *The Secret of Merging with Your Instructor's Mind*

In any school situation, what the instructor or lecturer says in the classroom may be as important as any single book or article assigned for reading.

Of course, some teachers communicate better than others. But it's wise not to be too quick to criticize any teacher or discount what he says in class. A major reason for listening closely is that even the most inept instructors will usually be directly involved in devising and grading your tests. Lectures are one way to determine how the teacher thinks and what he's likely to include on exams. So the better you can understand how your teacher's mind works, the more impressive your performance is likely to be on his tests.

Even under the best of circumstances, taking effective notes in class can be tedious. And the challenge with some disorganized lecturers may seem downright impossible.

## Julie's Great Challenge in Psychology Class

One of our students, Julie, was almost in tears. "I know I'm going to fail psychology!" she told her Evelyn Wood instructor. "I can't understand a thing the lecturer is saying in this course!"

To get a better idea of the problem Julie was facing, the reading instructor, Bob, made an appointment to attend the class with Julie. Just before the lecture began, they took seats together at the back of the room, and when the teacher arrived and began speaking, both began to jot down notes.

By the end of the class, Julie had filled four-and-a-half word-packed pages with paragraph after paragraph of sentences. Bob, in contrast, had constructed a slash recall pattern on one page.

As the other students were getting up to leave, Julie looked curiously at Bob's notes. But before they could really get into a conversation about his evaluation of the class or his technique, they looked up and found the lecturer standing beside them.

"Please sit down," the lecturer said, and Julie and Bob immediately fell back into their seats, expecting a reprimand. After all, Bob was something of an interloper.

After looking the instructor up and down a couple of times, the lecturer asked, "Okay, who are you?"

Bob gave his name and said he was from the Evelyn Wood reading program. "Julie's taking my class because she's afraid she's going to fail yours," he continued. "So I told her I'd come here and listen to you and try to help her with note-taking techniques for the lectures."

"What's that?" the psychology lecturer asked, pointing at the slash recall pattern.

"My notes," the reading expert said. Then, he proceeded to explain how a slash recall was structured and showed how the psychology talk fit on the different branches of the outline.

"When you began the lecture, you said you were going to talk about emotions," Bob said. "Then, you said you *weren't* going to talk about emotion, but you *were* going to cover motivation and eating, including why people are over-weight. You can see that here, here and here, I wrote down key words to remind me of what you were saying."

Bob's explanations were quite civil and polite. But as he talked, it became clear to all how disorganized the lecture had been.

Finally, the psychology lecturer, who was actually a teach-ing graduate student, broke in with some disarming hon-esty: "I wasn't very organized, was I?"

"Well . . ."

"Can you show me what I can do to give more organized lectures?"

That was a totally unexpected response. Bob recovered quickly and described how an organized talk might be con-structed with a slash recall pattern. The lecturer listened intently, asked a number of in-depth questions and actually practiced drawing several rough recall patterns, which Bob critiqued. As for Julie, she picked up the essentials of the slash recall, which she resolved to use in future note-taking.

After this incident, the lecturer's performance improved markedly. And Julie began to get much more out of the course—both because she was now employing the slash re-call and because her lecturer was using it. Bob, the Wood-Britannica instructor, never did learn how well Julie did on her grades, but apparently the problems that she had been experiencing with incomprehensible lectures were no longer a concern.

When I first heard this story, I had some trouble believing that a lecturer would have been so open about his deficiencies and so ready to alter his own note-taking and lecture style. Most teachers I've known would become rather defensive when confronted with even the indirect, gentle criticism that was offered in this encounter.

But this psychology lecturer really did want to improve, and his willingness to acknowledge his own flaws and try a new approach to organizing his lectures paid off.

Even if your teacher fails to change his or her ways in the classroom, you can still maximize your understanding and recording of key oral information. The secret: Simply employ the recall pattern techniques that Julie's reading instructor used.

How does this work? Much of what you've learned about using recall patterns with written materials will apply to lectures, but there are a few distinctive features that bear further discussion.


## How to Take Lecture Notes

Most students at one time or another fantasize about either using a tape recorder or shorthand to capture every word a lecturer says. But in fact, both of these fantasies are unrealistic.

In the first place, if you turn on a tape recorder with the intention of listening to the lecture again before the exam, you'll in effect have to double your lecture time. You'll not only spend twenty-five to thirty hours or more in the classroom; you'll also have to spend another twenty-five to thirty hours listening to the tapes. On top of that, at some point you'll have to take notes and study them. As for shorthand, you'd need to spend hours transcribing the symbols. Then, you'd have to sort through the verbatim text to find the nuggets you expect to be on the test. Multiply these time requirements by all your courses, and you can see why I say these approaches are unrealistic.

With such an exhausting, time-consuming prospect, it's not surprising that most students opt for the traditional approach: They simply take notes during the lecture, and then study those notes later for their exams.

But there's a better way to take lecture or discussion notes. Taking a cue from the instructor who visited Julie's psychology class, I'd suggest that you rely on the recall pattern concept. Keep these points in mind:

First, it's best to begin with the slash recall pattern because of its flexibility. If you discover later that the teacher's approach is such that a radial or linear pattern will work better, then feel free to switch.

(Note: In a very few cases, when a teacher is exceptionally well organized, the old-fashioned outline approach may turn out to be an efficient way to take notes. In other words, the teacher might actually read from an outline by saying, "I have five main topics, which you may want to put under five Roman numerals. Now, Roman numeral one . . ." But for the large majority of lectures—and all free-wheeling class discussion—the slash recall pattern is the best technique.)

Second, try to take one page of recall pattern notes for every hour of lecturing.

When you first attempt this approach with class presentations, you may find that you can't get everything on one page. In fact, it may take as many pages as you were using with the old outline or paragraph method. But with practice, you should develop the ability to put all the pertinent material on one page.

A word about the type of notebook you use: Most people keep their class notes in a letter-sized spiral notebook, but some students, especially those who like a little more room to operate, may use a legal-size pad to draw their patterns. You'll probably have to experiment to find which kind of paper is best for you.

You may have already noticed as you write on a slash or other type of recall pattern, that it's awkward to record notes on the branches that travel in a nonhorizontal direction on the paper. So when you find yourself writing in a cramped position, just turn the paper at an angle that allows you to write more easily. The more comfortable you feel taking notes, the more quickly you'll be able to write—and speed can be especially important in a fast-moving lecture.

Third, as the teacher begins to speak, listen to understand, not to record notes.

Your goal is to think, not just be a stenographer. Try to grasp the main ideas and facts first. Then jot down on the pattern a summary in your own words of what you've heard.

Among other things, you should pay attention to the following:

Note the logic and reasoning process the lecturer uses to make his main points. It's essential for you to understand how he gets from point $A$ to point $B$. This kind of thinking will promote your own ability to remember and will also place you in a position to make strong, cogent arguments on essay questions.

What examples is he using? Note them and fill in facts when necessary from your reading assignments. Then, plan to use these examples—which are obviously your teacher's favorites—on your tests.

Do you agree with her position? Be sure to add your own

134

opinions to the pattern as you go along. The more you can engage with the lecturer at this point, the more you'll understand and be able to use what you've heard. If you find you do disagree with something, you should try to get some answers from your teacher during class discussions or after the class sessions.

Fourth, when possible indicate connections between ideas and concepts on the pattern. For example, you might link related sets of branches on a pattern by drawing arrows and inserting a key word or two to indicate the connection.

Fifth, write down only main ideas, key words and essential data, not every little detail. As you jot down these major points, you might "talk" to yourself, continually evaluating and sifting the information you're hearing. If you have trouble understanding anything the lecturer is saying, include a question mark with an appropriate word at that point. Then, immediately after the lecture, you should ask the teacher to clarify the matter.

Sixth, be alert to ways of reworking the speaker's organization into a more logical format. To illustrate: You may find that you've included anger as a theme in a lecture on political revolutions. The lecturer may mention this theme several times in different locations in his talk. In this case, you might include a subsection entitled "Anger" in three different locations as the speaker did; but you may also set up a separate major heading for anger and place various relevant items under that heading.

Seventh, go over your recall pattern immediately after the lecture is finished. Think through and try to "talk back" the lecture, just to be sure you understand what was said. If necessary, fill in points that you failed to include while the speaker was talking. At this time, you may want to reorganize your notes or condense them on a separate sheet of paper.

The process of checking over and reworking your notes just after the lecture is an important part of the learning process. This reexposure to the material will help fix it better in your memory and make you more effective in later study.

Eighth, after you've checked your lecture notes following a class, schedule a reading and study session on the course material as soon as possible.

A lecture can be a useful warm-up for study. The more you immerse yourself in the subject through lectures *and* reading, the more complete your understanding of the material is likely to be.

Ninth, review your recall patterns regularly throughout the term. This way, you'll be in a better position to retain the information and retrieve it later to answer test questions.

Students who develop an expertise at using recall patterns for lectures and class discussions have several advantages over those who rely on extensive outline or paragraph styles of note-taking:

- Students using recall patterns no longer need to take such extensive notes because their approach encourages them to summarize what they hear.
- Even with shorter notes, they are likely to have more thoughts about the subject matter. Remember, you have to think before you can summarize a point in your own words.

  An aphorism frequently heard at the Evelyn Wood program over the years has been, "The less you know, the more you write." I certainly think this observation applies to lecture notes.
- Students who use recall patterns tend to respond with greater understanding to the teacher.

- They automatically develop an effective retrieval system for drawing on information later in preparing for tests. It's much easier to study lecture notes that cover only one page per hour of class time and are presented in a striking, graphically memorable format. (Some students have found that drawing a few impression-producing pictures or stick figures on their patterns can enhance recall during study.)

Finally, here's a model you may find helpful as you practice using the slash recall approach in your lectures. Some major headings, which apply to many lecture situations, have been included. But of course, you should change those headings as necessary to accommodate your note-taking to the particular class presentation.

## Model Slash Recall Pattern for Lectures

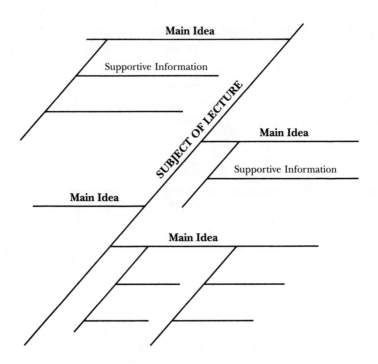

## *ACTION DIGEST*

**1.** Use a slash recall pattern for lecture notes.

**2.** Take one page of recall pattern notes for every hour of lecturing.

**3.** Listen to understand, not to record notes.

**4.** Indicate links between ideas and concepts on your recall pattern.

**5.** Record only main ideas, key words and essential data.

**6.** Rework the speaker's organization into a more logical format.

**7.** Review your recall pattern immediately after the lecture.

**8.** Schedule a study session as soon as possible after the lecture.

**9.** Review your recall patterns regularly throughout the term.

# 8

# *Supersonic Writing*

One of our new reading students, a high-school senior and honors candidate named Beth, had a block when it came to writing school papers. After putting off an assignment for weeks, she would finally begin to plod through the research materials at a snail's pace. Even a relatively short paper of four or five typed, double-spaced pages could easily require her to put in as much as two weeks of steady work to complete—if she allowed that much time for it.

More often than not, though, she would have less than a week and sometimes only two or three days available when she finally got started. As a result, she would typically stay up all night at least one night, operate under intense time pressure, and hand in a paper that was usually woefully inadequate.

In fact, Beth's poor performance on her written work was the major factor that periodically threatened to pull her down from her honors status. She knew that if she improved her grades on papers, she would be in contention for an even higher honors ranking than she now anticipated.

Beth finally lapsed into a state of near-panic after she received an assignment to write a paper at least 5,000 words long—or about twenty typed, doubled-spaced pages—on some topic of her choosing in her American history course. Detailed footnotes and documentation were required. Furthermore, the grade on this paper would count as one-third of her final grade for the course.

In desperation, Beth shared her problem with her Evelyn Wood instructor and asked for any help he could give her. At this point, she had attended several sessions of the Evelyn Wood reading and study course. But she couldn't quite see how the program was going to help her complete the paper that much faster.

In fact, though, our reading and study techniques can be adapted quite well to produce fast, supersonic writing on school papers. Here are the main stages in the research process that Beth's reading instructor described to her.

## Stage 1: Establish a Point of View

At the very outset of working on your paper, before you do any in-depth research or writing, you should determine the point of view you're going to take.

As you move further into the paper, you may adjust and change this viewpoint. But without an initial angle or orientation, you'll be at a severe disadvantage in producing a good piece of work. With an inadequately-thought-out theme, efficiency and speed in researching and writing a paper decline dramatically. In fact, you may end up with a completely disorganized piece of writing.

Here are some guidelines that will help you establish an initial point of view. As you employ this approach, it's helpful to draw a slash recall pattern containing branches with each of these major headings. Then, using the pattern, you can begin to think on paper by jotting down additional notes and sub-branches.

**Identify your general topic.** To settle on a topic for your paper, consider some of the possibilities from your general reading in the course. For example, Beth knew that she wanted to write about the pre–Civil War South, because she had enjoyed that part of the assigned reading the most. So she began to focus her thinking and additional preliminary reading on what she knew about this historical period.

**Define your specific theme.** Obviously, Beth's general topic had to be defined and limited. A twenty-page paper about the entire history of the antebellum South would be superficial, and frustrating to write. Volumes have been written about this subject.

So Beth began to narrow her topic down to a specific concept that was more appropriate for a 5,000-word treatment. Her goal: to be able to state her specific theme in one short phrase or sentence.

After referring to a couple of encyclopedias in addition to her textbooks and class notes, she decided that she would like to focus on the reasons the South had moved toward the conflict. Obviously, this was still a meaty subject. But it seemed limited enough to give her plenty of latitude for an in-depth discussion in a twenty-page paper.

Note: This process of defining a specific, limited theme may be the most important element in the successful research and writing of a school paper. So it's wise to take some extra time at this point to find just the right approach.

If your topic is too broad, you're going to get anxious and confused in attempting to organize and present too much material. But with a well-thought-out, appropriately delineated theme, you'll automatically be able to discard irrelevant research material and focus on your topic.

Being able to focus consistently this way on one viewpoint —an orientation that can be stated in a phrase or short sentence—is an invaluable organizing tool as you research, outline and write your paper.

**Anticipate the general research locations where you expect to gather facts.** Now that Beth had limited her theme to factors that caused the South to go to war, she knew that she had to target her research to a relatively limited time in history. She expected that her main work would involve library books, journal articles and other historical sources that dealt with the twenty to thirty years before the Civil War broke out.

As a kind of action plan, she included some notes on her recall pattern to identify major information sources. These included "school library"; "local public library"; "Mr. Jones's private records" (Mr. Jones, a friend of her family, was a Civil War buff); and "Civil War archives" (there was a special library and archive on the Civil War period near her home).

**At the outset, seek to develop your own opinions.** Every good paper includes the author's opinions about the subject under discussion. At this point, Beth hadn't come to any final conclusions about the reasons why the South went to war. But she had developed a few preliminary opinions from her class reading and lecture notes, which she recorded on her recall pattern. For example, she believed that Southerners' philosophical commitment to slavery was less important than the economic pressures they feared if they lost a source of cheap labor.

143

As you can see, the first steps in writing a good paper are quite similar to the initial purpose-setting and overview phases of efficient study and reading. Having a clear-cut viewpoint in mind will always make the student's life easier —and usually produce significantly better grades.

## Stage 2: Identify Specific Research Materials

Using the Multiple Reading Process, you should begin to examine relevant research materials at the various libraries and information locations that you've identified. At this point, don't try to complete all your research. Instead, conduct an overview of the books, articles and other materials that are available. You may also want to do some selective previewing of especially important books and articles, though actual reading should be postponed until later.

(In some cases, such as when there are severe restrictions on access to a library or other sources, you may have to go in and do all your research there on your first visit. But if possible, it's best first to get an overall idea of the quality of the materials available in different places. Then, you can go back and examine the most important information in more depth on a second visit or later visits.)

Here are some suggested steps to help you in identifying your sources.

First, arm yourself with appropriate materials. Buy some 3-x-5-inch cards to record the references you find. Also, you should carry a couple of larger pads for making more extensive recall patterns. And of course, don't forget to take at least two or three pens or pencils, in case the one you're using breaks or runs out of ink.

Second, develop a list of possible resources. Don't be

afraid to use your imagination. Also, check with librarians in charge of centers of information. They are usually highly trained in the way their library materials are organized, and they can often provide the student with advice about reader's guides, bibliographies and other sources.

Third, overview every book you find that seems relevant to your topic.

Fourth, if you think you'll use a particular book or article for your paper, record on your index cards all the essential information that you'll need for footnotes and bibliographical references.

You should learn *before* you begin your research what format your teacher requires for documentation so that you can get it all on paper at this stage. There's nothing more frustrating than to finish a paper and find you have to wade back through all your sources in various libraries simply because you forgot to note the publication date or some other essential element. In general, you'll need to record the full title, the author, the pages pertinent to the topic, the publisher and the date and place of publication.

Fifth, after overviewing the sources, begin to draw recall patterns.

It may be possible to put a recall pattern on the index cards for sources that are of relatively limited value or contain only a small amount of information. For more important sources, however, you'll probably have to use a larger sheet of paper for the recall pattern. If you do formulate a recall pattern on a second sheet at this point, be sure to copy the documentation information onto the recall pattern so that you'll have it handy later for inserting footnotes.

Sixth, in some cases, you may also want to preview some especially important books or articles at this preliminary stage. If you do, fill out your recall pattern further with the additional information you gather.

Seventh, as you take these preliminary notes and record your documentation, identify and note on your cards the sections of books and articles that you want to read in more detail later.

Eighth, limit the time you spend in this source-identification phase of your research! For a paper the length of the one that Beth had to write—about 5,000 words—one or at the most two days was plenty of time to devote to this preliminary stage.

## Stage 3: Compile All Your Information

Once again, the layering approach to reading and studying comes in handy as you do the main part of your research for a paper. The steps should be quite familiar by now, though some of the techniques must be adjusted to fit the special needs of different types of research.

Group your index cards according to each library or other location where the references can be found, and within each of these groups of cards arrange the sources in order of priority, from most important to least important. Probably the initial overview and preview you conducted of certain books or articles that seem least important will suffice. In that case, just put those cards aside for later use in writing the paper and listing sources in a bibliography.

In your primary research location—such as your school library—overview the most important book or article once again and formulate a slash recall pattern for it if you haven't done so already. After you overview this time, fill in additional information on your pattern.

Preview each section or chapter you've overviewed, and add to your recall pattern. Then read the section that you've just previewed and add more information to your recall pattern. While you read, keep the following two special considerations in mind. First, direct quotations you want to use in your paper may be copied at this point, with an indication of the page where they can be found in the text (for later use in footnoting). Second, if a publication has a great deal of important or densely presented information—such as a set of statistics or a listing of items or facts—you may even want to photocopy that page and attach it to the back of your recall pattern or index card. Postview anything you've read in the book or article that needs clarification.

Follow the procedure just described with the other publications in this primary research location, moving from the most important to the least important source. Then repeat this approach to compiling information in each of the other libraries or research locations that you've identified.

## Stage 4: Reorganize Information into One Master Recall Pattern

Now is the time to gather together the recall patterns and index cards on all the information you've compiled. Your objective is to use this raw material to formulate a master recall pattern.

Obviously, this master pattern, which will serve as your basic outline and guide for writing the paper, can't contain every detail that you've collected in your research. Rather, you should focus on the main topics and main subheadings.

As you draw the new, overall pattern, however, you'll probably want to refer somehow in your notes to the more detailed, smaller patterns that you've drafted. This way, you can prompt your memory about what idea or fact comes from what source. (Beth, for example, used a book by an author named Smith, so she made a couple of notations to Smith with appropriate page numbers.) In any case, be sure to save all your recall patterns and other notes so that you can use them as you work on your drafts of the paper.

Because this master pattern will contain many different concepts and ideas, you may want to draw it on an oversized sheet of paper. (Or, as you'll see in a later section describing an alternative approach used by a top teacher, you might link the various recall patterns together into a kind of scroll.)

For now, let's assume that you're drawing one master recall pattern on a large sheet of paper, with short notations that refer back to other recall patterns. When you've finished this phase, you're finally ready to begin writing.

## Stage 5: Write the First Draft

Now you're ready to begin putting your paper together. Here are some steps that have worked well for many of the most successful students.

First, assemble all the materials you'll need to do the draft. These include all your notecards, recall patterns, photocopied pages and other sources; enough pens, pencils and paper; and your typewriter or word processor, if that's appropriate.

As you already know if you have one, a word processor can be an invaluable tool when you begin to write. On most of these computers you can move text about, make inserts and deletions freely, and type more quickly with such advantages as the "wrap-around" feature, which eliminates the need to return the typewriter carriage.

Begin to write your draft by following the sequence you've chosen on your master recall pattern. Refer back to the supporting recall patterns and index cards when you need specific facts and quotations that you couldn't include on the master pattern.

To facilitate reading and editing, it's wise to learn to compose a first draft on a typewriter or word processor. Be sure to double-space and leave ample margins. If you write by hand, leave plenty of space between lines and wide margins so there will be adequate room to make editing notes and alter the text. Use this format on the final draft, too, so you can put the paper in a binder if necessary and also provide the teacher with room to write in comments.

Play it straight as you write. Don't try to be "literary" or use an affected, overblown style. The best writing is simple and clear, with a majority of sentences set in the active rather than the passive voice. Check Strunk and White's classic, *The Elements of Style,* for guidance.

Use plenty of paragraphs—preferably at least three or four per typed, double-spaced page. The more you break up the page with paragraphs, the easier it is for the instructor to read and understand your organization.

Each paragraph should deal with one major thought and should flow naturally and logically to the next paragraph. If a transition between paragraphs seems choppy, rewrite or insert a phrase or sentence to make the transition smoother.

Use sections, subsections and underlining when appropriate. Obviously, you don't want to overdo any of these text divisions. But as with paragraphs, an intelligently constructed set of subheadings or underlinings (to highlight important material) can make reading move along much more easily.

The basic structure for most papers includes the following:

1. An introduction, which states the main theme of the paper clearly. As some pundit once said, "Tell them what you're going to say; next, tell them; and finally, tell them what you've said." Obviously you don't want to be redundant; however, it's important in a paper to make it clear at the outset where you plan to take the reader.
2. The body of the paper, which includes each of your main points, with supporting facts and footnotes. It was in this section that our honors student, Beth, inserted the reasons that the South went to war. Remember to keep your paragraphs relatively short as you make your presentation.
3. The conclusion, which contains a summary of your main points. Be sure that the evidence you've marshalled supports your argument.
4. Documentation. Double-check all footnotes to be sure your citations and format are accurate. Also, prepare your bibliography.

Edit and proofread your first draft, paying close attention to your grammar, spelling and syntax. Also, check to see that your argument and presentation flow along smoothly. If any section of the draft seems rough, or doesn't seem to follow from the previous section, try to come up with a better transition. If you can't think of a good transition, perhaps you need to rethink the organization of the paper.

Postview the draft, asking yourself some important final

questions: Have I proved my basic thesis? Do I lack sufficient facts in any part of the paper? Does my overall organization seem natural, or does it seem artificial or strained? (If the organization isn't adequate, you may have to move your facts and points around, or you may even have to rewrite the paper. The best students are always ready to do a second or third draft if that seems necessary.)

## Stage 6: Prepare the Final Draft

If you've done a thorough job with your preliminary drafts, the final draft of your paper should be a cinch. Here are the suggested steps:

Arrange the paper in the following sequence for final typing:

1. Title page, including the title of the paper, your name and address, the date, the class designation and the name of the teacher.
2. Table of contents, if used, with chapters, section headings and page numbers (this feature frequently impresses a teacher).
3. Preface or introduction, if used.
4. The main text, with introduction, body and conclusion.
5. Footnotes (if they are placed at the end of the paper).
6. Bibliography.

Retype your paper in the above order; number the pages in order; and proofread the entire paper. Then turn it in —and expect a higher grade than you've received in the past.

## *How Fast Can You Write?*

How long should this entire process of putting together a lengthy paper take? In Beth's case, with a 5,000-word research paper, here are some realistic time expectations. (I'm assuming, by the way, that Beth can type at a rate of about 40–50 words per minute.)

- Preliminary thought, including choosing the basic theme: 1 hour.
- Identifying relevant books, articles and other research sources: 1 day (5 hours).
- Compiling information: 3–4 days (15–20 hours).
- Reorganizing the information and drafting a master recall pattern: 1–3 hours.
- First draft: 8–10 hours.
- Final draft: 5–6 hours.

Total elapsed time: 35–45 hours.

Now, this may seem a long time to devote to one paper. But remember: The written work in this particular case constituted one-third of Beth's grade.

Also, to research and write any paper of this length will take most serious students much longer than 35–45 hours, which is the equivalent of one intense week's work. Below-average students may devote less time, but they'll also get lower grades. I've plugged into this estimate the times required to do a truly top-flight job on a term paper.

As an alternative—and potentially an even speedier approach to paper-writing—consider the following "scroll" technique developed by one of our top instructors.

## *A Supersonic Case Study*

Before he discovered the Evelyn Wood method, our instructor Dan Warner was a different person. As an English major in college, he avoided classes which required term papers. He couldn't take all the extra reading he knew would be required before he sat down to write. "Even if only four or five extra books were necessary, I actually felt physically sick when I'd sit down to read the first book," he recalled. "I also knew I'd fall asleep trying to read."

But after he took the Evelyn Wood course, his academic life, including his paper-writing, was transformed. After spending a full day finding information in the card catalogue and periodical guide, he ended up with 104 books and 78 magazine articles as sources on his first post–Evelyn Wood paper!

Then, instead of relying on the traditional index-card method of recording information, he walked into the library with several legal-sized notepads and a shopping bag. As he found information he needed, he wrote his notes or recall patterns on the paper, ripped off each set of notes when he was finished, and tossed the sheets into his shopping bag. (As I've suggested in the previous section, he would always include a complete reference on the paper for later footnotes.)

"If at any point in this process a thought came to my mind that represented a developing personal opinion or insight, I'd jot it down, write 'Me' on it, rip it off and throw it into the bag with everything else," he said.

Finally, when he had compiled all his research information, he dumped his research materials out on the floor in his room and began sorting the notes and papers into clusters, according to the main topics on the master recall pattern. Dan formulated a brief master recall pattern so that he would have a clear statement in front of him of what the main topics in the paper would be. Also, he determined the order in which he wanted to discuss each topic.

When this clustering process was finished, he then lined up the clusters in the order in which he wanted to present them in the paper. Finally, he began stapling the papers to one another in their appropriate sequence, with the top of each attached to the bottom of the one preceding. (Clear tape would have done just as well.)

He placed several blank sheets of paper at the beginning and end of the connected notes and also some blank paper between each of his main topics. This way, he had space to draft a rough introduction and conclusion and also to include transition sentences or paragraphs between the main sections.

So what Dan ended up with was a continuous sheet of paper about twenty feet long. Then, to make it more manageable and portable, he rolled it up into a scroll. What he had as a result of this stringing together of his notes was a kind of first draft of the manuscript.

Finally, Dan went through his note-scroll—i.e., he "postviewed" it—to see if everything was in order. At this point, he also jotted in an introduction, his transitions, and a conclusion on the blank sheets of paper he had inserted.

There are a number of advantages to this scroll technique. Suppose, for example, that you forget to include any facts or observations. Or perhaps you have discovered some material at the last minute, after the scroll has already been constructed. In these situations, all you have to do is take some scissors, clip through the scroll at the appropriate point, and insert the new material with staples or tape.

Also, by using a scroll, you can put your research materials in precisely the order you want for your first draft. In fact, as I've already indicated, the scroll actually forms a kind of first draft.

Finally, when all one's notes are attached in sequence, there tends to be less rummaging around for misplaced materials as the drafting is being done. Furthermore, it's relatively easy to transport a scroll to a library or some other facility outside your room and do work there.

Now, with his scroll before him, Dan proceeded to type out his first draft. He began at the top of the scroll, where he had jotted in the introduction; unrolling the notes, he moved steadily through to the conclusion. His draft of this term paper was forty pages long, complete with footnotes and bibliography.

How long did it take him to write this first draft? Barely ten hours. That's four pages an hour—record time, when you consider that two to three pages an hour is often considered a good pace by professional writers.

"It was really just a matter of typing up what I already had on paper," he explained. "I didn't have to worry much about organizing the paper, inserting transitions or other such things. Those problems had already been dealt with as I was stringing my notes together. That scroll really did constitute a first draft for me."

At this writing pace, Dan would have completed the first draft of a twenty-page paper—the length that Beth wrote in our previous example—in only five hours. Or a ten-page paper could have been done in two and a half hours.

You can see the potential with this scroll approach, which is merely a fine-tuning of the basic supersonic paper-writing techniques that I've already described. In any event, whichever method you use, the main idea is first to overview, preview and read the research materials at your best speed.

Then, you should spend adequate time organizing your notes and recall patterns in some fashion. The better job you do during this reorganization and master recall pattern phase, the more quickly your drafting will go. That was the beauty of Dan's scroll technique.

Certainly, writing the paper requires time and thought. But effective writing is much like effective reading or studying: The more thinking and organizing you can do in advance, the easier it will be to reach supersonic speeds, whatever the academic challenge happens to be.

## *ACTION DIGEST*

In writing a class paper, follow these steps:

*1.* Establish a point of view.
*2.* Identify specific research materials.
*3.* Compile all your information.
*4.* Reorganize the information into one master recall pattern.
*5.* Write the first draft.
*6.* Prepare the final draft.

# 9

# *How Fast Can You Go?*

All the skills you've learned so far—including the hand motions, the layered reading process, and the various preparatory procedures for effective study—have been moving you inexorably toward this point. Now, you're ready to put it all together, to see just how fast and efficiently you can read and study.

In this chapter, you'll learn to hone the skills you've acquired and to break through to new plateaus of supersonic reading. Most likely, if you practice the "push-up" and "push-down" drills and other exercises described in the following pages, you'll find yourself identifying with one or more of these students:

**Anna.** As a junior in high school, Anna's reading rate was 330 words per minute, and her level of comprehension was 65 percent. She had become frustrated with her performance at school, which ranged from B-minus to C-plus. So, on her own initiative, she enrolled in one of the Evelyn Wood courses.

After only about one month of practice, her regular reading rate had risen to 1,440 words per minute, with a comprehension level of 85 percent. Even more important, her ·grades at school began to get better. She began to do much better on her tests, with grades consistently in the A-minus to B-plus category.

By the time Anna had finished her junior year, her mother had become more than curious about her marked academic improvement. "This is not the Anna I know," she told one of her friends. "She's always been one who was content just to get by. Maybe she's finally growing up."

But then, her mother began to put two and two together: "You know, I think it may be this reading course she's been taking. That seems to have changed things completely."

After Anna confirmed this analysis, the mother hit on a bright idea. She knew that her daughter had turned in a mediocre performance during her first two and a half years of high school, and those low grades were bound to work against her as she applied to colleges.

So she suggested—and the school guidance counselor supported—this novel strategy: Anna would write to her prospective colleges explaining how her study habits and performance had been transformed as a result of the Evelyn Wood methods. Also, the mother and counselor asked Anna's Evelyn Wood instructor to write a separate letter to the various college admissions committees.

The results were highly encouraging: The majority of the admissions officers said that they would take the changes in Anna's study habits into account in considering her admissions application. As a consequence, she gained admission to at least two schools that she would ordinarily not have expected to enter.

**Brian.** A seventh-grader, Brian, was assigned a two-hundred-page paperback novel to read for a test. The test

159

was scheduled in two weeks, and Brian was worried about his ability to handle this extra piece of work. Like that of most children his age, his schedule was loaded up with other homework and extracurricular activities.

Fortunately, however, Brian had been taking an Evelyn Wood reading and study course. As a result, he had acquired some important skills that enabled him to complete the reading assignment with relative ease.

Reading at a rate of about 1,000 words per minute, he completed the book in a total of less than two hours—and he did it on the same day that the teacher had assigned the book. The entire elapsed time even included the drawing of a rather complete slash recall pattern.

Then, on two or three evenings in the next two weeks, Brian reviewed his notes, reread some sections of the book, and added appropriate facts and comments to his recall pattern. By the time test day rolled around, Brian was completely prepared. He received an A on the test.

**Max.** Eventually, Max became the star pupil in a course given by one of our instructors, Carol Romaniszak. But he didn't by any means develop his stellar reading and studying capacities overnight. In fact, at the beginning of the program, Max complained several times, "I really don't get this stuff. I don't understand how I'm supposed to increase my reading speed this way. It just doesn't *feel* right to me."

The Evelyn Wood program can be like that at first: Some of the concepts may seem quite strange to new students. I liken our techniques to the first steps in learning skiing or tennis. During the first few tries, you may fall down, or miss the ball, or whatever. But eventually, for those who stick with it, these "strange" new sports become more familiar—and expertise and enjoyment increase.

Max started the program reading at a rate of 300 words

per minute, with only 48 percent comprehension. But he had made up his mind to work hard, and every time the instructor introduced a new concept that he didn't quite understand, he'd stop her and say, "Wait, wait a minute. Could you go over that again?"

Like a bulldog, he'd hang on to each skill that he found difficult until he finally understood it and began to master it. Then, invariably, he'd announce, "Yeah, I got it now. I've got it cold!"

In fact, Max learned everything so well that by the end of the three-week course, he had increased his reading rate to an incredible 2,927 words per minute. And his comprehension had soared to 92 percent!

These students, and many others like them, have experienced phenomenal improvements in their reading speeds and comprehension scores in our course. Furthermore, high achievement in the Wood program is consistently reflected in higher marks in schoolwork.

But I want to be completely realistic here. It's true that most students can see dramatic improvements in their reading and recall abilities with less than a month of intensive work. Commonly, reading rates increase from about 250 words per minute at the beginning of the course to 1,000–1,200 words per minute or more at the end.

On the other hand, these skills are just that—skills. A skill of any type, intellectual, social or athletic, will atrophy unless it's maintained with regular nurturance and practice. You can talk to many of our instructors and they'll tell you that they can read at their highest rates only when they're "in shape," or "in training," or "in practice."

Earlier in this book, I described some of the speed plateaus that can be reached through subvocal linear reading. As you may recall, there is a kind of supersonic subvocal barrier at about 800–900 words per minute for this type of reading. To break through this barrier, it's necessary to begin to read vertically and visually. This process becomes more possible as you use the various vertical hand motions, layering methods and other techniques that have already been described.

What can you expect in terms of speed and experience after you do break through the subvocal barrier? Here are some of the possibilities.

## Beyond the Subvocal Barrier

After a student moves through the subvocal speed barrier of about 800–900 words per minute, he usually hits a range of reading that can best be described as rough.

Specifically, when the student's rate varies between about 900 and 1,200 words per minute, there's a tendency to shift back and forth between subvocal linear reading and visual-vertical reading. As the pace moves up toward and above 1,200 words per minute, however, the style of reading becomes more consistently visual-vertical.

But it's often difficult to maintain a regular pace above the 900-word-per-minute barrier. And inevitably, when the reading rate slips below the barrier, subvocal linear reading takes over.

In some ways, this problem is analogous to a challenge that may confront an airplane pilot. Pilots are instructed about the stall speed for their aircraft: If the plane's forward progress is allowed to drop below that speed, the engine may cut off. Similarly, the reading "engine" that allows you to soar at high visual-vertical speeds will shut down if you reduce your speed below the subvocal barrier.

Certainly, I think it's a great achievement even to reach the point where the dominant movement of your eyes down the page is visual and where most of the information you're taking in is going directly from your eyes to your brain, without being routed through your vocal cords. But it's important for every student to know that the reading range just above the subvocal barrier, in the 900–1,200-word-per-minute zone, is a transition spot. You really must push yourself beyond the 1,200-word-per-minute range if you hope to reap all the benefits that the visual-vertical techniques can provide.

So what's the next plateau, above this transition range?

Most experts agree that the goal for the majority of students should be to read consistently at a rate above 1,500 words per minute. At this pace, you're able to process all the words and thoughts on the page and also to generate new thoughts and opinions of your own. You can take in the gestalt of the reading material without at the same time missing important details. In addition, you don't have to worry too much about slipping into that transition zone below 1,200, which may tug you further down, into a subvocal linear rate.

It's important to note, as I've indicated in earlier chapters, that "reading speed" or "reading rate" refers only to the reading phase of the layered or multiple-exposure study process, not to the overview and preview that should precede the actual reading.

As you already know, the overview and preview steps don't take very long; usually, about a second a page is required for those experienced at overviewing, and no more than three to four seconds a page for the preview. But these first two phases of study are absolutely essential to achieve the highest reading rates.

Of course, it's possible to move well beyond the 2,000-

word-per-minute range, but then something different beings to happen. In the 2,000–3,000-word range, for instance, you'll acquire a broader view of the material as you see more clearly how the sections of a book fit into each other. On the other hand, it's not as easy to pick up details in the reading.

As your speed goes even higher, perhaps up to 4,000–5,000 words per minute, you're limited more to the broadest general impressions about the book. (The major problem many readers confront is how to turn the pages fast enough.)

Think about it for a moment: Reading at 5,000 words per minute in a book that contains about four hundred words per page would require the student to read more than twelve pages per minute, or nearly a page every four seconds. That doesn't leave much time for fumbling with pages that get stuck together.

As a matter of fact, it's really not clear whether what takes place at these high speeds should be described as traditional reading or something else. What's different about these very high speed plateaus?

In the first place, studies haven't confirmed whether those who can move at this pace are seeing every word on the page, though in many cases their comprehension scores stay high. Also, there may very well be a different mental process that comes into play at the fastest speeds. Some readers who have moved up to 5,000–10,000 words per minute or beyond have even reported near-mystical sensations.

One of our managers and top instructors, David Hardwick, began reading at a rate of 250 words per minute. Then, after taking the basic Wood course, he found that he could move along comfortably at a rate of about 2,500 words per minute with most nonfiction. His speed with fiction was even faster—about 4,000 to 6,000 words per minute.

On the other hand, as he explains it, the entire reading process involves dynamic movement at a variety of different speeds, depending on one's objectives and the nature of the subject matter.

"The only time you might lock into one speed and use it continuously is when you're in the process of taking an examination. Otherwise, you adjust your speed according to the material and your level of familiarity with it.

"In other words, I may have the ability to read at 3,500 words per minute in marketing material. But you put a medical book in front of me, or a lawbook, and I'm going to have to start at a much slower pace because the language will be relatively unfamiliar."

When he reaches the higher rates of speed, though, he reports that a "very definite sensation . . . occurs." He notes that a reasonably sustained visual-vertical experience for him starts to occur in the 900–1,500 range. Above that level, the physical sensation that he referred to becomes a factor.

"Once, in practicing the preview technique, I began to read at an extremely high rate—a rate that was later clocked at about eleven thousand words per minute. Going that fast, I lost my sense of self. There was no more 'Here's David practicing the preview technique.' Instead, I became totally immersed in the material. Pages later, I suddenly came to myself and realized that I had been involved in some sort of meditative experience."

Typically, when a person becomes so involved in the reading process, the memory intensifies. He can recall much more of what he's read than is possible under ordinary circumstances. Also, as David indicated, there is little or no awareness of the process of reading. Rather, the student begins to experience directly the message the author is conveying through the words.

Those who reach these higher plateaus of reading usually say they see and understand more of what's on the page than they do when reading at slower speeds. The "structure words" in the book—i.e., the main verbs, nouns and connective words that convey the meaning of the text—seem to leap off the page and into the student's mind and feelings.

Perhaps all this sounds too mystical for you, and certainly, it isn't necessary to partake of such a total immersion in a book to get the full benefits of it for academic purposes. But I'm interested now in outlining some of the ultimate possibilities.

In some ways, what David Hardwick and others have described may be similar to the whole-brain experience to which others have referred. According to a number of recent studies and theoretical discussions, the right and left sides of the brain have a major impact on how we perceive and experience the world around us. In right-handed people, the left side of the brain is believed to control those mental functions relating to language, logic, mathematics, fact-finding and analysis. The right half of the brain, in contrast, focuses on broader, intuitive, visual, spatial and nonverbal mental functions.

How do these ideas relate to reading?

A number of observers have said that subvocal-linear reading is all "left-brain." That is, this slower type of reading centers mostly on the logical, word-by-word progression of thought on the written page.

Visual-vertical reading, in contrast, is said to pull the more intuitive right brain into the process. When this happens, the brain can not only evaluate and interpret the material logically but can also see the total flow of the text. The mind is no longer limited to the word-by-word order of thoughts on the page; the eyes and mind are freed to move faster, and high-speed reading and study become possible.

Whatever the correct explanation for what happens when a student reads at the highest speeds, it's clear that something distinctive does indeed occur. But now the question for you is, "How can I experience this kind of Mental Soaring? How can I reach my maximum possible speed?"

## Pushing Beyond Your Speed Limit

The first rule for those who want to increase their reading rate to the maximum possible speed is *practice*. No one, not even our top instructors, can hope to maintain the highest levels of visual-vertical reading without regular "workouts."

For example, Carol Romaniszak admits that her reading rate falls to 1,000–1,200 words per minute, with 80 percent comprehension, when she's not "in training." On the other hand, when she *is* in training, she works regularly at speeds of 2,000–3,000 words per minute with high levels of comprehension.

But how do you push your speed limit up to these higher plateaus and keep it there?

The first answer to this question is that you should read and read and read. And as you read it's essential to employ the techniques I've been describing in this book. Granted, they may seem strange at first. But believe me, the more you use them, the faster and more efficiently you'll find you can go through printed materials.

There are also some drills that we've found extremely

helpful in first pushing your speeds up to higher plateaus. In general, we classify these in three ways: push-down drills, push-up drills and power drills.

**Push-down drill.** Push-down drills increase your reading rate and at the same time build up your comprehension rate. Here's how they work:

1. Pick a text that you've been assigned in one of your humanities or social studies classes. Place a watch or clock with a second hand nearby so that you can easily glance up from the text and note the time without significantly interrupting your reading pace.
2. Using the underlining hand motion, read for one minute in the text. Then, place a paper clip at the spot where you stopped reading. Compute your words per minute and write this figure down on a separate sheet of paper. (See page 16 for a refresher on doing this computation.)
3. Using the underlining hand motion again, read the same material in fifty seconds. You *must* reach the spot where you placed the paper clip in this period of time. (As you can see, you're "pushing down" the time it takes you to read a given segment of text.)
4. Now, shifting to the S hand motion, read the same material in forty seconds. Again, you must reach the paper clip.
5. Using the S motion again, practice the same material in thirty seconds.
6. Next, switching to the question-mark hand motion, practice the same passage in twenty seconds.
7. With the question-mark motion again, practice through the same text in ten seconds.
8. Now, using a hand motion of your choice, begin reading

in the text at the spot where you placed the paper clip and see how far you can get in this new material in one minute. Place a paper clip where you stop, and compute how many words you've read in the new material. Chances are, you'll find you're reading at a significantly faster rate than you were when you began the drill.

Here's a variation on this drill which can add a gamelike dimension to study: Do the push-down drill by devoting ten minutes to each step instead of just one. Then, if you really feel ambitious, you might try the exercise in fifteen- or twenty-minute segments. Most likely, you'll find yourself flying through your assignments, with increased comprehension and efficiency.

**Push-up drill.** The purpose of this exercise is mainly to increase your speed, rather than your comprehension.

Using this technique, you learn, first, what it feels like to move at significantly faster reading rates. Second, you get a sense of the eye and hand motions necessary to enable you to read quickly. Once you've developed these skills and become familiar with the process of faster movement, you can expect higher comprehension levels to follow.

1. Using the underlining hand motion, read for one minute in a school text, and place a paper clip at the spot where you stop reading. Again, be sure to have a watch with a second hand near your field of vision so that you can easily keep track of the time. Count the number of words you've covered in this minute. This figure is the number of words per minute at which you're currently reading.
2. Now, using the underlining motion once more, start at the beginning again and read for one minute at a faster pace. You should move through the old material and get

well into some new material within the one-minute time limit. Advance your paper clip to the spot in the text that reflects the new speed record you've achieved.

3. Switch to the S hand motion, and reread again at an even faster rate, beginning at your original starting point in the text. As in the second step, place your paper clip at the new, more advanced spot in the text where you've stopped.

4. Now count the pages from the place where you started reading, to the spot where you last placed your paper clip. Next, count off the same number of pages into new material in the text and put a second paper clip at that point. In other words, the second paper clip should mark a point at double the number of pages that you've been able to read so far.

5. Using the S hand motion, practice for one minute at a pace that will take you to the second paper clip. You must reach that second clip, even though you most likely won't understand much of what you're trying to read. But still, allow your eyes to move over all the words on each page, and pick up as much as you can.

   Remember, your goal now is speed, not comprehension. If you're like most of our other students, you can expect a comprehension rate of only about 10–20 percent at this point.

6. Now, you're ready for some real supersonic mental soaring. Count off a segment of pages beyond your second paper clip equal to the segment before the first clip. Place a third paper clip at this point. In other words, you'll now have three clips in the text at equal distances from one another.

7. Using the S hand motion, practice for one minute, beginning at your original starting point in the text. Again,

you must reach the final, third clip in this one minute. As in the fifth step, your comprehension of the newest material will be low, this time probably less than 10 percent. But when you finish this step, you will have tripled your speed over what you achieved in reaching the first paper clip.

8. Finally, it's time to see what this push-up drill, which has been primarily designed to stretch your speed capabilities, has done for your overall reading ability. Using a motion of your choice read for one minute in new material in the text which lies just beyond your third and final paper clip. Move along at a pace that seems fast, but still allows you to pick up the general concepts, thought patterns and significant details in the text.

Now, compute your words per minute in this new material. You should find that you are reading considerably faster than you were when you began the exercise.

A variation on this drill: Instead of limiting your time segments to one minute, increase them to ten minutes each. As in the push-down drill, this approach with homework assignments can inject a gamelike quality into studying and should enhance speed and efficiency in completing homework.

**Power drill.** This exercise is intended mainly to build up your ability to comprehend and recall what you've read.

1. Choose an assigned text from one of your classes, make sure you have a pencil and some paper handy and place a watch or clock with a second hand near your line of vision.
2. Using the question-mark hand motion, move quickly

171

through the text for one minute at a preview rate (about four seconds per page).

3. Close the book and for another minute, recall everything you've previewed. Jot down what you remember on your paper on a recall pattern.

4. Using the S hand motion, read as quickly as you can for one minute, beginning at the point in the text where you started your preview. Don't worry if you don't pick up everything, or even most things, in the text at this point. Now you're trying for speed as much as for comprehension.

   Keep in mind that it's highly unlikely that you'll get as far with this reading as you did with the preview.

5. Close the book and for one minute recall all that you've read. Add those recollections to your recall pattern.

6. Using the S motion again, reread for one and a half minutes from your starting point. This time move at a somewhat slower pace that will allow you to pick up more of the ideas and details in the text. But you should still be pushing yourself to the limit, concentrating on speed as well as on comprehension.

7. Close the book, recall all you can for one minute, and add what you remember to the recall pattern.

8. Using the S motion once more, reread again from the beginning, this time for two minutes. Your pace now should be one that will allow you to pick up the details you need for your normal study purposes.

9. When you're finished, put the book aside again and spend another minute recalling what you've read. Include this additional material on your recall pattern.

10. Finally, compute the word-per-minute rate of your final, two-minute reading in the ninth step. That figure will represent how fast you were reading with full comprehension.

A variation on the power drill: Increase the preview and reading time segments by ten times their original values. In other words, the preview in the second step would take ten minutes instead of one minute; the first reading in the fourth step would take ten minutes instead of one; and so forth. Your recall times should stay about the same as they were in the original exercise, though you can lengthen them by as much as an extra minute if you like.

Fast and efficient reading and study are possible for everyone, but the maximum rates—and the most powerful study tools—will always be reserved for those who are willing to drill and practice. As a general rule, the exercises I've described above are most useful for those who haven't yet reached their maximum speed, or for those who are out of practice and need a refresher.

Students who have moved up to the higher speeds—more than 1,500 words per minute with at least 70–80 percent comprehension—can usually stay there simply by reading and studying regularly, while using the Mental Soaring techniques I've already described. In fact, many people find that if they read for even an hour a day using these methods, they steadily increase their speeds automatically, with high comprehension.

But in the last analysis, where are all these study guidelines and speed-enhancing techniques taking us? For a student, of course, the bottom line is the final examination. So our last major topic must focus on how the skills you've been acquiring so far can be applied in a testing situation.

## *ACTION DIGEST*

***1.*** Reading speeds higher than about 1,200 words per minute can be achieved only with a visual-vertical approach.

***2.*** The overview and postview are essential prerequisites to achieve top reading speeds.

***3.*** Practice with push-down, push-up and power drills is necessary for reaching the highest speeds and rates of comprehension.

# 10

## *The Thrill of the Final Test Flight: Using Your New Skills to Ace the Exam*

For the average nonstudent, the skills that we've been considering in this book can be used in a variety of ways: reading professional periodicals; researching speeches or other oral presentations; perusing office memos; studying formal reports; breezing through the daily mail; previewing and reading general background materials, such as newspapers; or pleasure reading, including the latest best-seller.

But for students, the ultimate goals are a little different. All reading and study are eventually intended to fulfill two main objectives: completing assigned papers and taking tests.

We've already explored how to use the Evelyn Wood techniques to research and write papers. But another weighty, grade-determining topic still remains—the issue of successful test-taking.

Let's separate the examination issue into two parts: first, the question of pretest preparation; and secondly, the challenge of the test itself.

# Pretest Preparation

In our work with students over many years, several key principles have emerged for effective pre-test preparation. Here are the main ones that you should know and follow.

## Principle 1: At All Costs Avoid Cramming

Much of what has been said up to this point has centered on the importance of regular, relaxed reading and study. Earlier in this book I advised you to read all your assigned books and articles in the first two weeks of the quarter or semester, and at that time to set up recall patterns on all this reading. Then you should concentrate on reviewing your recall patterns at regular intervals, and when necessary should reread especially tough or important materials well before examination time arrives.

This way, you will improve your memory of the material over the course of many weeks and months, to the point where you gain great familiarity and facility in evaluating and discussing it. Such an intimate understanding of school assignments is an important prerequisite to maximize one's success on tests.

Cramming, in contrast, involves gaining only a temporary, superficial grasp of required books and articles. Furthermore, trying to take in an entire semester's course work in only a day or two can be exhausting and may dull the mental acuity necessary to do one's best on a test.

To be sure, some students can get very good grades after a cramming session. But they could do better—and certainly would enjoy learning much more—if they substituted the methods I've been describing for last-minute cramming.

Of course, you will want to intensify your studying in the day or two before an exam, just to be sure that the important facts and concepts are at your fingertips. But there's a way to go about this without increasing stress levels and triggering panic.

I've included below a "test inventory checklist" that we recommend our students use when they are in the final phase of studying for an exam. But note that it's best to finish the process described in these points before the day immediately preceding the test. On that last day, as we'll see shortly, the best students generally follow a somewhat different procedure.

So here are some suggestions about what to do during the pretest preparation period up to, but not including, the last day before the exam:

One, recall what's been discussed most in the class. You should be able to identify these points from your recall patterns. Then, be sure you know this information cold— because it's quite likely you'll see some of it on the test.

Two, taking each text or other piece of assigned reading in turn, check to see that you know the most important points, dates, terminology or principles, as highlighted by the author.

Three, either on paper or out loud, define all the new words, ideas and thoughts emphasized by your teacher or by the various authors in the course reading. You may have heard these words and concepts so often that you think you know them. But in fact, you can't be sure you can give an adequate definition or description unless you actually do it.

Four, jot down all the questions you can think of that your teacher might ask. Then, try answering aloud each of the questions you've posed. Many students find it's also helpful to draw a brief recall pattern containing the key points remembered during these talk-aloud sessions.

Five, when you review your materials, try to explain in your own words what you've learned. By rephrasing what you've read, you'll accomplish two things. You'll make the information your own by demonstrating to yourself that you really understand what you've read. And you'll prepare yourself to give a fresh version of the information on the test. Teachers prefer that students explain assigned materials in their own terms, rather than just parrot back the facts and concepts in the author's words and phrases.

A couple of exceptions to this point: Often there are central, landmark terms and phrases in a field of study that you should echo in your examinations and tests, just to show that you are familiar with basic knowledge or important developments in that field.

For example, you'll undoubtedly find you have to use precise terms like "genus" and "species" when you're writing an essay on those topics for a biology exam. Also, it probably wouldn't be wise to write a test answer on England's Glorious Revolution of 1688 without using the term "Glorious Revolution."

Also, you may want to use the author's own words—or for that matter, your teacher's own words—when you're including a direct quotation on a test. A short (and important) direct quote on a test, with an appropriate citation of its source, can impress many teachers.

Six, review all the conclusions that your teacher and the authors you've read have made. Some of these are likely to be called for on your test.

Seven, in the last day or so, concentrate mainly on reviewing your recall patterns. Your main objectives should be to fix the overall sweep of the course clearly in your mind, and also to check your memory of the major topics and subtopics.

When you're presented with a question on the exam, you

should be in a position to "file through" your memory and pick out the facts and concepts you need to respond to the test question. The best way to do this is to memorize the overall structure of the course, a structure which will be reflected on your recall patterns.

At this time, you may also want to refer back to your textbooks or other sources for any points that you've left off your recall patterns. This is your last chance to do this, and don't be discouraged or panic if you find some rereading is necessary. Remember, you now have the skills to check books quickly to gather additional information.

## Principle 2: Take Aggressive Measures to Manage Pre-exam Anxiety

Some of the most gifted students fail to do their best on exams because they become excessively nervous just before the test. On the other hand, a good student may also perform below par because he fails to get nervous enough!

When you're too nervous, you tend to freeze. Your mental processes become blocked; things that you normally would remember easily simply won't come to mind; creativity disappears; and panic frequently sets in, thus making the situation even worse.

At the other end of the spectrum, a tired, lethargic, bored, depressed or negative-thinking student may seem to lack nerves at all. But that's not because he's relaxed. Rather, he's given up before he even enters the examination room! Lacking the competitive edge required to do his best on a test, he also ends up performing far below his capacities.

So what's needed is a feeling of nerves that lies somewhere between these two extremes. I know many top students who worry if they're not feeling edgy or having butterflies in the stomach before a test. On the other hand, they've learned to manage this pre-exam anxiety so that it doesn't get out of hand and begin to paralyze them and inhibit superior performance.

How do these students manage their nerves before an exam? Here are some practical tips we've gleaned from evaluating their approach:

**Avoid answering questions of other students during the day before the test.** That's not to say that you should become antisocial, or refuse to interact to some extent with your classmates in an effort to pick up points you may have missed. But the best students generally find it's counterproductive to try to verbalize in-depth answers to questions in the minutes or hours just before the test.

One reason is that many people tend to fixate on a last-minute concept or question that's posed to them. In other words, that particular issue may loom so large that it becomes difficult or impossible to draw on other material studied.

Also, trying to answer last-minute questions from classmates, especially when the queries require a great deal of thought, may actually make it more difficult to respond to a similar question on the test. The student seems to exhaust his ability to deal with a particular question or issue when he focuses on it too much just prior to the exam.

Finally, trying to answer questions at the last minute can trigger panic. Almost any other student is capable of posing some question to you that you feel you can't answer adequately. When this happens, a typical response is, "Oh, no, I don't know this material at all! These other guys are much better prepared than I am."

In fact, though, the questions that other students put to

you just before the exam are not likely to be on the test, at least not in the form that the classmate has chosen. Furthermore, responding off the cuff as you're talking to someone outside a test situation doesn't provide you with an opportunity to put your best foot forward. After all, most people put out their best effort when they know it counts. In addition, you'll almost always do better when you're able to see the questions on paper in front of you, rather than when you're trying to deal with an issue off the top of your head.

But be sure to keep this piece of advice in perspective. As I've indicated earlier, it *is* a good idea to try to anticipate questions that your teacher will pose on the test and also to do some trial runs in trying to answer those questions. This practice testing, however, should be done well in advance of the test, or at least several days ahead of time, so that you'll have an opportunity to work through all the possible answers for potential questions *and* have a day or so to sit back, review the entire course, and be certain you have the big picture in mind.

**Admit to yourself that you may not know all the answers to the test.** This confession of one's limitations can be a truly freeing experience. So many of us, either consciously or subconsciously, assume that we have to know everything for an exam. Then, when we find, as we almost always do, that we don't know everything, we experience panic or despondency, and test performance declines.

So it's best to approach a test with this thought in mind: "Some of the things on the test I'll know, and some I won't know. But everyone is going to be in my situation, so what I have to do is just try my best and trust that what I do know will far outweigh what I don't know."

**Continue normal, healthy daily habits on the last couple of days before the test.** If you think about it, most of your life is probably relatively relaxed or at least characterized by a certain emotional evenness. High anxiety is not the typical emotional status for most people.

To manage the normal feelings of nervousness and worry that accompany examination periods at school, you should find it helpful to continue to do what you normally do on a typical day—provided that these activities are healthy.

Suppose you usually devote some time each day to exercise, chatting on non-school topics with friends, watching the news on television or perhaps praying or meditating. If such are your habits, continue with them right up through the last day before the test.

Also, it's extremely important to eat a normal, healthy diet. Too many students either disrupt their normal eating habits or skip key meals, such as the breakfast before the exam, with the result that they run out of energy just before or during the test. Others may decide to coddle themselves by splurging on rich or fatty foods. As a consequence, their digestive tract has to work overtime, and a mental sluggishness sets in. Both extremes are to be avoided.

A familiar routine, in itself, can help calm the mind and contain excessive test anxiety. But whatever you do, the goal should be relaxation and reduction of unnecessary stress. A movie on the evening before a test may even be a good idea for some people.

On the other hand, it's not a good idea to stay up too late, take drugs or get drunk on the day or night before the test —even if those are part of your normal routine. Those activities will just dull your mental faculties, make you feel guilty or irresponsible, and aggravate feelings of anxiety or inadequacy. In general, during the twenty-four hours preceding the exam, stay away from any activities that make you depressed, put you in a negative frame of mind or in any way have the potential to upset you.

Finally, get up early enough on the day of the exam so that you can get dressed, eat and walk to the test site without rushing. Plan on getting to the site ten to fifteen minutes before the time when the exam is scheduled. Any earlier may make you nervous anticipating the test; but any later can also increase anxiety.

## Principle 3: Operate at the Test Site as You Have When Studying

Test day is not the time to try new approaches to writing, new ways of staying alert or innovative academic skills. A seasoned tennis player would never try to play an important match with a new racket without first practicing with that racket and learning all its characteristics and peculiarities. Instead, he would rely on the racket and other equipment that had worked for him in the past. Similarly, a student should stay away from untried techniques or unusual practices that may throw him off stride in taking the test.

For example, if you've been studying and taking tests with a pencil and paper in the past and you're just learning how to type, you should stick with the pencil and paper. Eventually, after you've gained experience with a portable typewriter or word processor, or with typewriters or word processors provided at the test site, these tools can be extremely helpful in taking exams. But for the inexperienced under the time pressures of a school exam, they can quickly lead to disaster.

I'd also suggest that if you've become accustomed to

183

drinking coffee while you study, you should have some coffee just before you take your test. Or, if it's allowed, you may want to bring a cup into the exam room.

In general, whatever habits you've observed while studying, try to bring them into the exam room as much as possible. This familiarity with certain study tools and habits will enhance your ability to perform at a maximum level, and will also help reduce test anxieties.

Now, with these preliminary preparations out of the way —and motivated by just enough nervousness, but not too much—you're ready to take your final test flight.

## The Final Challenge: A Short Philosophy of Successful Test-Taking

The best test-takers usually embark on their examination with a plan firmly rooted in a philosophy based on their prior successes with tests. Here it is:

**Overview the entire test.** The idea here is to get a feel for the exam: how long it is, what type of questions are being posed (e.g., essay, multiple choice, matching) and which questions seem easy or hard.

Sometimes in this preliminary phase, you may even stop and jot in an easy answer on a short-answer question. But generally, the idea at this stage is just to get the big picture or gestalt of the test, as you would during the overview of a book.

**Read all the directions on the test closely.** Too often, an intelligent, well-prepared student will do poorly on a test because he misses or misreads some key instruction. To give you an idea about how important it is to read directions, try doing the following exercise, which has been used in a number of our classes. (You can do any necessary writing on a separate sheet of paper.)

**Directions:** Do exactly as instructed. Under no circumstances are you to speak or ask a question. Be sure to keep your eyes on your own paper. When you have finished, sit quietly until everyone has finished this drill.

1. Read everything before you do anything.
2. Proceed carefully and cautiously.
3. Put your name in the upper right-hand corner of this paper.
4. Circle the word "Name" in sentence three.
5. Draw five small squares in the upper left-hand corner of this paper.
6. Put an "X" in each square.
7. Put a circle around each square.
8. Sign your name in the lower right-hand corner of this paper.
9. After your name, write yes, yes, yes!
10. Put a circle around each word in sentence number 8.
11. Put an X in the lower left-hand corner of this page.
12. Draw a triangle around the X you put down.
13. On the reverse side of this paper, multiply 703 by 1,850.
14. Draw a rectangle around the word "paper" in sentence number 3.
15. When you get to this point in the test, snap the fingers of your left hand.
16. If you think you have followed directions up to this point, write "I have" in the space provided below.
17. On the reverse side of this paper, add 8,950 and 9,850.
18. Put a circle around your answer. Put a square around the circle.
19. Shut your eyes for just a few seconds. Then proceed to line 20.
20. Now that you have finished reading carefully, do only sentence three.

It's amazing to watch the people in our classes dealing with this test of discernment. Usually, only one or two will actually read through, get to number 20, and only write their name in the upper right-hand corner of the paper. Most become engaged busily in drawing squares, Xs and circles, snapping their fingers and doing the arithmetic problems.

Unfortunately, too many people take school tests the same way. They never really read the directions closely, and as a result, they make all sorts of unnecessary mistakes on their exams. Yet as this test clearly demonstrates, reading those directions and following them to the letter is absolutely essential for those who hope to become superior test-takers.

**Allocate and organize your time.** The third thing that most top students know as they enter the test room is that it's necessary to set aside a few moments for time management. To achieve the best time management on a test, however, it's important to focus in more detail on the kinds of questions that the test maker has given you.

## Some Tips on Taking Specific Types of Tests

There are two basic types of tests that students usually have to deal with in school: objective or short-form tests and essay tests. The objective tests can generally be subdivided into four categories—true/false; multiple choice; matching items; and completion or direct answer.

To begin with, here are a couple of general comments that apply to all objective tests: First of all, read the directions carefully. Second, look over the entire exam and determine which items are easiest and which are hardest. Many students like to answer the easy questions as they go over the test during this preliminary stage. Then, they come back and spend more time on the harder items.

Here are some guidelines about how to tackle each of the test types.

## True/False Questions

1. As you read the instructions, be especially alert in determining where you're supposed to put your X or check. Does it go next to the true or the false item?
2. Ask before you begin the test whether or not you're penalized for wrong answers (i.e., are wrong answers subtracted from the right ones?). If you're not penalized, you should feel free to guess. If you are penalized, guessing should be severely limited.
3. Mark statements true only if they are *absolutely* true (unless your instructions indicate that you should mark those that are "mostly" true).
4. Be wary of statements with special or absolute words. For example, those with words like "never," "always" or "no one" are likely to be false. Extreme statements are almost always false.

## Multiple-Choice Questions

In this type of test, you're asked to select the correct answer from a group of given answers. Many vocabulary tests, for instance, are multiple choice.

One major advantage for the student with this kind of test is that the correct answer is always given. As a result, the shrewd student can often find the right response simply by process of elimination.

On the other hand, it's just as important to read the directions carefully with multiple-choice tests as with any other type of exam. Too often, for instance, students will assume that on a vocabulary test, the question is calling for a word with the same meaning (a synonym), when what's really needed is a word with the opposite meaning (an antonym).

Sometimes, the student can find the correct answer by asking a series of questions about the item. This kind of self-questioning can help clarify what the question is really asking and can assist you in eliminating obviously wrong answers.

Here's an example:

A selfish person is:

1. puny
2. young
3. vulgar
4. wealthy
5. egotistical

In thinking through the question, you should note that because of the way it's phrased, using "is" instead of "may be," a selfish person *must have* one of the listed characteristics. It's not enough that he *might* have one or more of them. So you could pose these questions:

Is a puny person *always* selfish?
Is a young person *always* selfish?
Is a vulgar person *always* selfish?
Is a wealthy person *always* selfish?
Is an egotistical person *always* selfish?

Clearly, the first four statements aren't true. That leaves only the last statement as the correct answer to the test question.

## Matching Tests

Matching tests have items listéd in two columns. The first column might be a list of terms, and the second a list of definitions. Each item in the left column must then be matched with the correct item in the right column.

The following steps can help test-takers improve their performance on this type of test:

1. Check to see if there are the same number of items in each column. Often, the right column will contain more items than the left. But you're in luck if the numbers are equal. It's always easier to answer matching questions when there are the same number of items in both columns.

2. Select the first item in the left column, and try to find its matching partner in the right column. Then, record the number of the matching item in the appropriate place, draw a connecting line between the items, or follow other instructions you've been given.

   If you are only supposed to write the number of the correct item in a box next to the left-hand list, be sure to check off that item on the right-hand column before you move on to the next one. Otherwise you may give the same answer twice. In any case, by checking the items off, you can tell quickly which ones remain, and that will speed up your completion of the test.

3. Match all the items that you are sure fit together.

4. Match all the items that you think might fit together.

5. Finally, check the left column once more to see which items are left and match those with the right-column items that remain.

6. Keep moving! The chances are that mulling over questions of this type won't enhance your ability to arrive at

the right answer. And if you're "stuck" on a question for too long, you'll just reduce your chances of getting the right answers on later items.

## Direct Answer or Completion Tests

This kind of exam is quite popular with teachers because the questions are relatively easy to formulate and also they test your knowledge somewhat better than other objective exams. Among other things, direct answer tests don't provide you with the right answer, as does the multiple choice approach. You are the one who has to come up with the correct response by filling in the blanks.

Here's a sample:

_____ invented the cotton gin.

If you don't know that Eli Whitney invented the gin, you won't have the luxury of taking a guess from a list of possibilities.

Some tips on taking this kind of test successfully:

1. Sometimes a direct answer test will just ask a question, and you'll be expected to provide a short response. Here are some key words to keep in mind if you get this type of test:

   "Who . . . ?" calls for a person or people.
   "Why . . . ?" calls for a reason.
   "How . . . ?" calls for certain steps or procedures.
   "What . . . ?" calls for facts.
   "When . . . ?" calls for a date or time.
   "Where . . . ?" calls for a place.

   It's also helpful to use the above words to rephrase questions that require you to fill in the blanks. You may be able to narrow the field of correct answers somewhat by asking which of six questions apply to a particular item.

Take the example I gave for a fill-in-the-blank question. You might rephrase it by asking, "Who invented the cotton gin?" Many times, restating the question will bring the answer to mind.

2. Again, be sure you understand the instructions for the direct answer test. A case in point: If the question calls for *one* name or word and you give *two,* you'll be wrong.

3. Sometimes, the length of the line you're supposed to fill in may give you a clue to the answer. Also, the number of broken lines may indicate the number of words. But try to ascertain from the directions or the instructor whether these factors are really signaling what they seem to be signaling.

4. Be sure to place your answers in the right spot. If you fill in the wrong blanks or put the answers in the margin, you may miss every item!

## Essay Tests

Essay questions often strike the greatest dread in the hearts of students. Some fear that they "don't write well enough to ace this kind of test." Others are afraid because "essay tests are so open-ended! I never feel sure I have the right answer or approach."

But students who have prepared properly have little to fear—so long as they tackle these questions systematically. Here is a basic plan:

**Step 1.** Know and identify the key "action" or "clue" words that characterize essay tests.

When you see one of these words, underline it and start

your mind working in the appropriate direction. The key words include the following:

- "Explain." The teacher wants you to answer the question by telling what a particular principle or process is, how it operates and how it works.
- "Describe." The teacher expects you to give a word picture of the appearance of an item or concept, its nature or some process identified in the question.
- "Discuss." You must describe the arguments for and against the issue or point described in the question.
- "Define." The teacher wants the exact meaning of the term or word. A one-line or one-word definition usually won't do.
- "Compare." Your instructor wants you to describe the stated ideas, people or events briefly and then show how they are alike and how they are different. When you're organizing your answer, it should be acceptable to divide it into these three parts: 1. the basic descriptions of the items; 2. the ways they are alike; 3. the ways they are different.
- "Enumerate." The teacher wants you to list every point as though you were counting them. Generally speaking, unless the instructions say otherwise, you should just list your points without giving details.
- "Prove." This word calls on you to give evidence, facts or figures to show that what you say in the essay is true.
- "Outline." The teacher wants you to list only the important ideas, and to group the less important, supportive ideas under them.
- "Evaluate." You're required to give the points for and against a stated position or situation. Then, you should state your own personal opinion or conclusion.

192

- "Summarize." The teacher wants you to write a brief statement of the main points, but you're not to go into detail.

**Step 2.** Preview each of the essay questions.

Assume, for example, that there are seven questions, and you're to answer four of them in an allotted time of two hours.

Using your fast previewing techniques, you should go over each question with an S or question-mark hand motion. Then, after you complete your preview of each question, draw a brief slash recall pattern and fill in the main relevant points you'll need to answer the question. The pattern might be drawn in the margin or on a separate sheet of paper. Do this for all the questions, even though you'll eventually only select four.

How long should it take to complete this process of previewing and drawing brief slash recalls on all the questions? I generally recommend that you devote about one-fourth to one-sixth of the total time for the test. So in our example, with a total test time of two hours, you should spend about twenty to thirty minutes on this preview.

Why do a slash recall for all the questions?

First, it's difficult if not impossible to evaluate your knowledge of a question without doing some serious thinking about it—and that usually necessitates putting something down on paper.

Assume that you just glance over the questions and make your selection too soon. You may find later that you actually had much more information on one of the questions that you initially discarded, simply because at first glance it seemed too tough.

Second, a seemingly easy question may turn out not to be

easy because you don't have any solid information to back up your opinions and conclusions.

So it's best, in effect, to take the whole test—albeit rather quickly! This will be time well spent because you'll be in a position to evaluate all the questions and select the ones that are really best for you.

**Step 3.** Using your recall patterns as a guide, select the four questions that you think you can answer best.

**Step 4.** Establish a time schedule for the rest of your test.

Let's carry the above example a little further. You have two hours to do your essay exam, and you've already spent about a half hour getting settled and doing your slash recall patterns on all seven of the questions. Also, you've selected the four questions you're actually going to answer.

What do you do with the remaining hour and a half? First, determine the total number of minutes remaining, a figure which you'll quickly calculate to be ninety minutes.

Now, set aside twenty minutes to postview your answers, or check them over for spelling, style and general sense at the end of the test period.

That leaves you with seventy minutes to write your essays. So divide that seventy minutes by four (the number of questions you have to answer), and you'll find that you have just under eighteen minutes for each question.

**Step 5.** Begin to write, using your recall pattern as a guide.

You may find that you'll have to add a few points to your recall patterns as you start to draft your answers, but only spend a second or two making a notation on the pattern as a reminder. Your main purpose now is to get that essay down on paper.

As you write, organize your answer as simply as possible.

It's usually best to divide the essay into three parts: a brief introduction; a body, containing all the major points and supporting facts; and a brief conclusion, which may consist of a summary of the major points and a final statement of your personal opinion.

It's very important at this stage to stay within the time limits you've set for yourself. Most students who fail to establish a time schedule spend more time on the first question or two than they do on the others. As a result, they run out of time at the end—and get lower grades.

It's all right to exceed by a minute or two the time limit you've set on a question. You may want to finish an important thought, and you do have some leeway because you've built in a twenty-minute time cushion at the end of the test. But don't encroach too much on your schedule. Otherwise, you may find you don't have any time at the end to revise, edit and postview your answers.

Think about it this way: If you write five minutes too long on each of your four questions, that will take up twenty minutes, or the entire time you had set aside for your postviewing. Or if, as many students do, you really neglect your time discipline and run over by ten to twelve minutes on each of the first three essays, you won't have any time at all to write the final essay.

Some students, on hearing this advice about the time management of essay tests, object, "But why organize things so that you have less than eighteen minutes to write each of the four questions? After all, the test lasts for two hours— why not spend a half hour on each question?"

Again, think about the entire procedure we've just been through:

First, you've actually spent more than eighteen minutes on each question because you've devoted the first half hour to thinking about each of the questions and writing recall patterns. Also, by doing an in-depth evaluation of each of the questions, you've put yourself in the strongest position to pick the best four.

Imagine how deflating and frustrating it can be to write four essays and be completely out of time—but then to realize that you should have picked one of the other questions. Sometimes, students come to this depressing realization after they've left the exam hall, and they spend hours or even days in self-recrimination: "Why didn't I *think* in that exam? Why didn't I read all those questions carefully?"

The approach I'm suggesting will greatly reduce the possibility that you'll be plagued by such second thoughts.

**Step 6.** Postview and edit your essays.

During the final twenty minutes you've set aside, proofread each essay for correct grammar, spelling and punctuation. Incomplete sentences, omitted words and misspellings will detract from your grade.

Also, during this phase you may discover you've omitted a key point. But there's no reason to panic. You have plenty of time, so just go ahead and insert the missing item.

These suggested guidelines for taking tests aren't by any means intended to be the last word on this subject. There are a tremendous number of helpful resources on the market that explain how to take all sorts of exams, from those in the classroom to standardized tests like the SAT.

The main point I've tried to get across here is this: The very same tools and techniques that you've been learning for more effective reading and study can also be applied to taking tests.

After all, you have to read all your examinations, even those on technical or scientific topics. Also, you frequently have to draft outlines for your answers, as when facing essay questions, and recall patterns are made to order for this task.

Much of this book has focused on setting objectives, establishing basic strategies and employing practical techniques for study. If you can carry the same mind-set into a test situation, you should be pleasantly impressed with the final results.

## *ACTION DIGEST*

Pre-exam principles:

**1.** Avoid cramming at all costs.

**2.** Manage pre-exam anxiety.

**3.** Operate at the test site as you have when studying.

**4.** Overview the test.

**5.** Read all instructions closely.

**6.** Select appropriate techniques for each of the different types of tests: true/false, multiple choice, matching, direct answer or completion, and essay.

# 11

# *Shooting For the Stars*

I've realized in presenting the ideas and techniques in this book that there are limits on how much one can convey through the printed page. At many points, I've wished that I could call you up or knock on your door and say, "Hey, do you really understand what I'm getting at?" or "You know, you have to practice that hand motion and that layering. It may take only a few minutes to learn a technique, but to master and maintain it demands regular attention." I've wanted a number of times to inquire about your developing skills. Are you excited about the potential of supersonic reading and study? Have you already experienced some successes in your schoolwork?

I'd like to hear about your progress. Even though I may not be able to speak to you face to face, please feel free to write to me with your reactions to this program. Here's my address:

> Dr. Stanley Frank
> Encyclopaedia Britannica
> 310 So. Michigan Ave.
> Chicago, IL 60604

If you would like more information about Evelyn Wood programs and classes, please call the Britannica Learning Centers at 1-800-447-READ. At the centers, you'll find instructors and other experts who can answer your questions.

The things you've learned in this book should have increased your reading speed significantly up to this point, and your comprehension should also be relatively high. For that matter, these new skills may very well have pushed your reading rate into the Mental Soaring range, in excess of 1,200–1,500 words per minute.

But there's more to the adventure of supersonic studying. For one thing, as you use these tools regularly, you'll find that you can develop personalized variations that enhance your enjoyment and improve your performance.

I've already mentioned in the discussion of the standard hand motions that once a student has mastered the basics, he should feel free to begin developing his own techniques.

Hence, some students have moved from the S to the crawl, which involves "creeping" the fingers quickly down the page. Others get to the point where they just move their finger down the margin of the book instead of using the sweeping motions I've described. Needless to say, this is a more subtle movement that is less likely to draw attention in a public place than the more dramatic standard Wood techniques.

But whatever methods you finally settle on, your performance is bound to trigger questions and comments. Many people will do a double-take if you turn the pages of a book every few seconds in their presence. (After all, most people spend a couple of minutes per page on a normal-sized book.)

Also, I've had reports from students using one of our pictorial recall patterns, who find they have to answer a barrage of questions from classmates, teachers or colleagues:

"What are you doing on that paper? It looks like hen scratching!"

"You're supposed to be taking notes, not drawing pictures!"

"I finally figured out that you're taking notes, but does that approach really work? Where did you learn how to do that?"

Despite the increased attention, most of our students find they're more amused than offended. It can be a lot of fun to put on a performance in front of fellow students or other friends—and know at the same time that the tools you're employing have greatly increased your capacity to take in and recall important information.

You've been introduced to a set of techniques that can revolutionize your ability to read quickly, recall more and achieve better grades. Now, it's up to you to see just how high and fast you can fly.

# Index

academic plan, 11, 42–66
  for final two weeks before tests,
    61–64, 66
  forty-minute formula in, 54, 66
  for last night before tests, 64
  for last three days before tests,
    63–64
  for preparing short papers, 60–
    61, 66
  relaxed study rhythm rule in,
    56–60, 66
  study space in, 46–50, 66
  term or quarterly schedules in,
    50–52, 66
  time management in, 50–64
  two-week rule in, 54–56, 66
  weekly schedules in, 51–54,
    66
academics:
  causes for problems in, 8
  improving performance in, 158–
    61
  skills needed for success in, 3–4
  speed-reading skills applied to,
    13–15
adults, mini-lessons for, 33–37
anxiety, pre-exam, 179–83, 198
auditory reassurance, visual
    reassurance vs., 69–71, 87

background noise, 49–50
background reading, 59
Basic Essential Skills Test (BEST),
    12

books, breaking in of, 27, 41
Britannica Learning Centers, 4, 6,
    13–14
  telephone number of, 200
brush hand motions, 105, 108

Camus, Albert, 34, 36
Carter, Jimmy, 7
chairs, selection of, 26
children, mini-lessons for, 32–33
class discussions, 11
  meshing studying with, 58–59
  note taking for, see lecture-note
    taking
class papers, 140–57
  anticipating general research
    locations to gather facts for,
    143
  basic structure for, 150
  bodies of, 150
  clustering process in, 153–54
  compiling all information for,
    146–53, 157
  conclusions of, 150
  defining specific themes for,
    142–43
  documentation of, 145–46,
    150
  establishing point of view in,
    141–44, 157
  five-day technique for writing of,
    60–61, 66
  identifying general topics for,
    142

class papers (*cont'd*)
  identifying specific research
    materials for, 144–47, 153,
    155, 157
  introductions of, 150
  preparing final draft of, 61, 151,
    157
  reorganizing information into
    master recall patterns for,
    147–49, 154, 156–57
  scroll technique in, 152–56
  seeking to develop own opinions
    in, 143
  time required for, 152
  writing first draft of, 60–61,
    148–51, 154–55, 157
clocks, layered reading compared
  to looking at, 70
clustering process, 153–54
completion tests, 190–91
comprehension:
  improvement of, 158–59, 161
  layered reading levels of, 79–
    80
  power drills to build up, 171–
    74
  push-down drills to build up,
    168–69
  at very high reading speeds, 164
cramming, avoidance of, 176–79,
  198
crawling hand motions, 106, 200

daily habits, test-taking and, 182–
  83
desks, secluded, 47–48
dialogue, subvocal linear reading
  of, 22, 41
diet, test-taking and, 182
direct answer tests, 190–91
discussion classes, *see* class
  discussions
documentation, 145–46, 150
double-checking, subvocal linear
  reading in, 22, 41
*Dune* (Herbert), 22

editing:
  of essay test answers, 196
  of first drafts, 150
Education Department, U.S., 8
effective reading, meaning of, 3
*Elements of Style, The* (Strunk and
  White), 149
English courses, two-week rule
  applied in, 55–56
essay tests, 12, 191–96, 198
  editing answers on, 196
  establishing time schedule for,
    194–95
  key words in, 191–93
  postviewing in answering
    questions on, 194–96
  previewing questions on, 193–94
  selecting questions to answer in,
    194–95
  slash recall patterns as guides to
    writing answers in, 194–96

fear, 31, 80
fiction:
  radial recall patterns for, 124
  relaxed study rhythm rule for
    reading of, 57
fill-in-the-blank questions, 190–91
final drafts:
  in academic plan, 61
  of class papers, 61, 151, 157
first drafts:
  in academic plan, 60–61
  of class papers, 60–61, 148–51,
    154–55, 157
  editing and proofreading of, 150
  formats of, 149
  in scroll technique, 154–56
five-day technique for writing class
  papers, 60–61, 66
5,000 to 10,000 words per minute,
  164
footnotes, 145
foreign language courses, two-week
  rule applied in, 55–56
forty-minute formula, 54, 66

400–600 words per minute, ix, 24
4,000 to 5,000 words per minute, 164
furniture, 48–49

gestalt:
in layered reading, 73, 82, 87
of tests, 184
goal setting, 75
memory enhanced by, 42–45
question-asking approach in, 43–45
reading speed related to, 165
*Green Mansions* (Hudson), 39, 105

half-moon hand motions, 105–6, 108
hand motions, 11, 88–108
brush, 105, 108
concentration enhanced by, 36, 89, 109
crawling, 106, 200
faster reading assisted by, 89, 109
functions served by, 29, 88–89
half-moon, 105–6, 108
horseshoe, 103–4, 106, 108
L, 101–2, 108
loop, 99–100, 108
pacing of, 17–18
in power drills, 171–72
in previewing essay test questions, 193
procedures for, 30
in push-down drills, 168–69
in push-up drills, 169–71
question-mark, 95–96, 106, 108, 168, 171–72, 193
regression discouraged by, 89, 109
S, 92–94, 107, 108, 168, 170–72, 193, 200
U, 104–5, 108
underlining, 24, 29–30, 35–36, 41, 89–91, 108, 168–70
X, 97–98, 108
Hardwick, David, 164–66

Hawthorne, Nathaniel, 126
Hemingway, Ernest, 126
Herbert, Frank, 22
hidden voice, 19–31
fine-tuning of, 23–31
*see also* subvocal linear reading
history courses, two-week rule applied in, 55–56
horseshoe hand motions, 103–4, 106, 108
Hudson, W. H., 39, 105

index cards:
in compiling information for class papers, 146–47
in examining research materials for class papers, 144–45, 155
in reorganizing information into one master recall pattern, 147
in writing first drafts, 148–49
instructors:
asking questions of, 59–60
communication abilities of, 129
determining manner of thinking of, 129–32, 134–35
during mini-lessons, 32–33

jokes, subvocal linear reading of, 22, 41
journalistic articles, radial recall patterns for, 124

Kennedy, John F., 7
key words:
in essay tests, 191–93
in lecture-note taking, 135, 139

language courses, meshing class sessions with studying in, 58–59
law books, linear recall patterns for, 124
layered reading, 11–12, 68–87
accepting visual reassurance in, 69–71, 87
advantages of, 84

layered reading (*cont'd*)
case study on, 80–85
comprehension levels in, 79–80
in examining research materials for class papers, 144
five steps in, 73–78, 87
foundations of, 68–80
overview in, 74–75, 79, 81–82, 87, 95, 104, 106, 114, 116, 144–46, 155, 163, 174, 184, 198
peripheral vision in, 72–73
postview in, 12, 54, 78, 80, 83, 87, 150–51, 154, 194–96
in preparing for tests, 78, 81–85
preview in, 54, 75–76, 79, 82, 87, 92–93, 95, 104, 106, 115–16, 145–47, 155, 163, 165, 172–74, 193–94
reading in, 76–78, 87, 104–5, 107, 115–16, 146–47, 155, 172–73
reading vertically in, 71–73, 87
review in, 78, 80, 85, 87, 95, 135–36, 139, 178
seeing and accepting words and phrases out of normal, expected order in, 68–69, 87
talk-out-loud technique in, 70–71
time allotment in, 78–79
understanding gestalt of what you read in, 73, 82, 87
lecture classes, 11, 58
lecture-note taking, 129–39
immediate reviewing and, 135–36, 139
indicating connections between ideas and concepts in, 135, 139
listening to understand in, 134–35, 139
notebooks for, 134
for psychology courses, 130–33
at rate of one page for every hour of lecturing, 133, 139
regular reviewing and, 136, 139

reworking speaker's organization into more logical format in, 135, 139
and scheduling reading and studying sessions, 136, 139
slash recall patterns for, 130–39
techniques for, 132–39
writing down only main ideas, key words, and essential datas in, 135, 139
Lees, C. Lowell, 37–38
left brain, subvocal linear reading related to, 166
legal cases, slash recall patterns for organization of, 122–23
L hand motions, 101–2, 108
diagram of, 102
execution of, 101
lighting, 26
in study space, 48–49
linear recall patterns, 124, 128
model of, 117
for taking lecture notes, 133
literature courses, random recall patterns for, 126
loop hand motions, 99–100, 108
diagram of, 100
execution of, 99

marginal notations, 77, 83
master recall patterns:
creation of, 147–49, 154, 156–57
in scroll technique, 154, 156
in writing first drafts, 149, 156
matching tests, 189–90, 198
mathematics courses, two-week rule applied in, 55–56
memory:
and adding emotional elements to reading, 43–44
and establishing reading goals, 42–45
note-taking skills for enhancement of, 45–46
*see also* recall patterns

memory plans, relaxed study
    rhythm rule in, 57
Mental Soaring, x, 3–41
    case studies on, 9–11, 13–15
    first step toward, 19–41
    foundation for, 4, 69
    gaining confidence for
        application of, 85
    implications of, 11
    preliminary steps in, 15–18
    techniques of, 71
Mill, John Stuart, 38–39
mini-lessons, 32–37
    for adults, 33–37
    for children, 32–33
multiple-choice questions, 187–88,
    198
Multiple Reading Process, *see*
    layered reading
music, 49–50

Nixon, Richard, 7
noise, background, 49–50
nonfiction textbooks, slash recall
    patterns for, 120
notebooks, recording lecture notes
    in, 134
note-taking skills, 14, 109, 201
    to assist in recalling important
        information, 45–46
    *see also* recall patterns
novels, radial recall patterns for,
    124

1,500 words per minute, 163
1,200 words per minute, visual-
    vertical reading in achievement
    of, 162–63, 174
optional reading material, 59
outlines:
    skeletal, 76
    *see also* recall patterns
overview, 74–75, 87
    in case study, 81–82
    in compiling information for
        class papers, 146

comprehension in, 79
drawing recall patterns after,
    114, 116
as essential in achieving highest
    reading rates, 163, 174
in examining research materials
    for class papers, 144–46, 155
horseshoe hand motions in, 104,
    106
question-mark hand motions in,
    95
in test-taking, 184, 198
time consumed in, 163
U hand motions in, 104

page-turning, 164
    efficiency in, 27–29, 41
    techniques for, 28–29
paintings, layered reading
    compared to viewing of, 70
parents, mini-lessons and, 32–33
participatory reading, 28
peer pressure, 13
peripheral vision, 72–73
photographs, layered reading
    compared to viewing of, 70
phrases out of normal, expected
    order, 68–69, 87
pictorial recall patterns, 125, 128,
    201
    model of, 119
Poe, Edgar Allan, 126
poetry, subvocal linear reading of,
    21, 41
points of view, establishing, 141–
    44, 157
    anticipating general research
        locations to gather facts for, 143
    defining specific themes in, 142–
        43
    identifying general topics in, 142
    seeking to develop own opinions
        in, 143
postview, 12, 54, 78, 87
    in answering essay test questions,
        194–96

postview (cont'd)
  in case study, 83
  comprehension in, 80
  of first drafts, 150–51, 154
  in scroll technique, 154
power drills, 171–74
pre-exam anxiety, 179–83,
  198
preview, 54, 75–76, 87
  in case study, 82
  in compiling information for
    class papers, 146–47
  comprehension in, 79
  drawing recall patterns after,
    115–16
  as essential in achieving highest
    reading rates, 163, 174
  in examining research materials
    for class papers, 145–46, 155
  horseshoe hand motions in, 104
  in power drills, 172–73
  question-mark hand motions in,
    95, 106
  of questions on essay tests, 193–
    94
  S hand motions in, 92–93
  time consumed in, 163
  U hand motions in, 104
  at very high rates of speed, 165
proofreading, 150
psychology courses, taking notes in,
  130–33
push-down drills, 158, 168–69, 174
push-up drills, 158, 169–71, 174

quarterly schedules, 50–51, 66
question-asking approach, 43–45
question-mark hand motions, 95–
  96, 106, 108, 168, 171–72, 193
  diagram of, 96
  execution of, 95

radial recall patterns, 124–25, 128
  model of, 118
  for taking lecture notes, 133
random recall patterns, 126, 128

reading:
  acquisition of skills in, 6
  adding emotional elements to,
    43–44
  awareness of, 165–66
  background, 59
  in comfortable environment,
    17
  dominant characteristics of, 20
  effective, 3
  establishing purpose for, 42–45,
    66, 75
  in groups of words, 18
  layered see layered reading
  optional, 59
  participatory, 28
  for pleasure, 79
  regression during, 18, 30–31, 41,
    89, 109
  subsonic, 12, 19–41
  subvocal linear, see subvocal
    linear reading
  supplementary, 59
  of test directions, 184–86, 198
  thinking compared with, 9
  visual vs. auditory reassurance in,
    69–71, 87
  visual-vertical, see visual-vertical
    reading
reading speeds:
  according to one's objectives and
    nature of subject matter, 44,
    165
  average, ix, 9, 11, 17
  calculation of, 11, 16–17, 32, 36,
    168–69, 171–72
  exercises to identify current, 6–7
  between 5,000 and 10,000 words
    per minute, 164
  between 400 and 600 words per
    minute, ix, 24
  between 4,000 and 5,000 words
    per minute, 164
  hand motions related to, 89, 109
  importance of, 8–9
  improvement of, 158–59, 161

above 1,500 words per minute, 163
above 1,200 words per minute, 162–63, 174
plateaus in, 161–62
power drills to increase, 172
push-down drills to increase, 168–69, 174
pushing beyond your limits in, 167–73
push-up drills to increase, 169–71, 174
reasons for increases in, 36
between 600 and 900 words per minute, 24
for subsonic reading, 24–25, 41
for subvocal linear reading, 24–25, 161–62
beyond subvocal linear reading barrier, 162–67
between 200 and 400 words per minute, 24
above 2,000 words per minute, 163–64
recall patterns, 11, 26, 55, 76, 110–28
advantages of, 113, 136–37
computer spreadsheets compared to, 112
in examining research materials for class papers, 144–45
formulation of, 114–16
functions of, 110–11
information on, 112–13
kinds of, 116–19
in layered reading, 82
in lecture note taking, see lecture-note taking
linear, 117, 124, 128, 133
master, 147–49, 154, 156–57
ordinary study notes vs., 112
pictorial, 119, 125, 128, 201
in power drills, 172
in pretest preparations, 62, 176–79
radial, 118, 124–25, 128, 133

random, 126, 128
in reorganizing information into one master recall pattern, 147–48, 154, 156–57
slash, 11, 113–14, 117, 120–23, 126–28, 130–39, 146–47, 160, 193–96
uses of, 113
in writing first drafts, 148–49
regression, 18
hand motions and, 89, 109
in subvocal linear reading, 30–31, 41
relaxed study rhythm rule, 56–60, 66
rereading:
comprehension in, 80
in layered reading, 77, 83
of marked sections, 77
at rate of subvocal linear reading, 84
of required assignments, 59
research materials:
anticipating locations of, 143
identification and examination of, 144–47, 153, 155, 157
research papers:
layered reading in preparing for, 78–79
see also class papers
review, 78, 87
in case study, 85
comprehension in, 80
of lecture noters, 135–36, 139
in pretest preparations, 178
question-mark hand motions in, 95
right brain, visual-vertical reading related to, 166–67
Romaniszak, Carol, 160, 167
Roosevelt, Theodore, 38

science courses, two-week rule applied in, 55–56
scientific texts, linear recall patterns for, 124

scroll technique, 152–56
  advantages of, 154–56
  clustering process in, 153–54
  first drafts in, 154–56
seclusion, 47–48
second drafts, 61
S hand motions, 92–94, 107, 108,
    168, 170–172, 193, 200
  diagram of, 94
  execution of, 92
  shopping lists, slash recall
    patterns in organization of,
    120–21
short-answer tests, 12
shorthand, lecture notes taken in,
    132–33
600–900 words per minute, 24
skeletal outlines, 76
slash recall patterns, 11, 113–14,
    120–23, 126–28
  advantages of, 120
  in compiling information for
    class papers, 146–47
  examples of, 114, 117, 137–38
  flexibility of, 133
  as guides in writing answers to
    essay test questions, 194–96
  for lecture notes, 130–39
  for legal cases, 122–23
  organizing shopping lists with,
    120–21
  in preparing for tests, 160
  in previewing essay test
    questions, 193–94
speed reading:
  academic applications of, 13–15
  benefits of, 14
  proof of, 37–38
  Wood's research on, 38–39
Stranger, The (Camus), 34, 36
Strunk, William, Jr., 149
study groups, 63
studying:
  meshing class sessions with, 58–
    59
  test-taking and, 183–84

study skills, 8–9
study space, 46–50, 66
  assembling all necessary study
    materials before beginning in,
    49
  devoted entirely to task at hand,
    48
  good lighting and furniture in,
    48–49
  inadequate, 46–47
  quiet, secluded table or desk for,
    47–48
  soft background noise or music
    helpful in, 49–50
subsonic reading, 19–41
  barrier of, 12
  hidden voice in, 19–31
  maximum speed for, 24–25, 41
subvocal linear reading, 20–22
  ability to see page in, 25–26, 41
  active page-turning in, 27–29, 41
  avoiding regression in, 30–31, 41
  basics of, 25–31, 41
  breaking in books for, 27, 41
  comfortable environment for,
    26–27, 41
  left brain related to, 166
  reading speeds beyond barrier
    of, 162–67
  rereading at rate of, 84
  speed plateaus in, 24–25, 161–
    62
  talk-out-loud technique vs., 71
  uses for, 21–23, 41
  using hand motions in, 29–30,
    35–36, 41, 89
  visual-vertical reading vs., 23
  see also hidden voice
supplementary reading, 59

tables, secluded, 47–48
talk-out-loud technique, 70–71,
    177
tape recording lectures, 132
term schedules, 50–51, 66
  sample of, 52

tests, 14–15, 175–98
  admitting to yourself that you
    may not know all answers to,
    181
  allocating and organizing time
    during, 186
  answering questions of other
    students on day before, 180–
    81
  brush hand motions in preparing
    for, 105
  continuing normal, healthy daily
    habits on last days before, 182–
    83
  cramming for, 176–79, 198
  direct answer or completion,
    190–91
  of discernment, 186
  essay, 12, 191–96, 198
  Evelyn Wood methods applied
    to, 159–60
  finding out format and emphasis
    of, 62
  last night before, 64
  last three days before, 63–64
  layered reading in preparing for,
    78, 81–85
  matching, 189–90, 198
  multiple-choice, 187–88, 198
  operating at test site as when
    studying for, 183–84, 198
  overviewing of, 184, 198
  philosophy for success in, 184–
    86
  preparations before, 61–64, 66,
    78, 81–85, 105, 160, 176–84,
    198
  reading all directions closely on,
    184–86, 198
  reworking recall patterns and
    other notes taken during
    school term for, 62
  short-answer, 12
  slash recall patterns in preparing
    for, 160
  study groups in preparing for, 63
  taking aggressive measures to
    manage anxiety before, 179–
    83, 198
  test inventory checklist in
    preparing for, 177–79
  tips for final two weeks before,
    61–64, 66
  tips on taking specific types of,
    186–96
  true/false, 187, 198
  vocabulary, 187–88
textbook material:
  slash recall patterns for, 120
  subvocal linear reading of, 21,
    41
thinking:
  average rate of, 9
  of instructors, 129–32, 134–35
Tolstoy, Leo, 124
true/false tests, 187, 198
200–400 words per minute, 24
2,000 words per minute, 163–
  64
two-week rule, 54–56, 66

U hand motions, 104–5, 108
underlining, 77
underlining hand motions, 24, 89–
    91, 108, 168–70
  diagram of, 91
  execution of, 89–90
  in mini-lessons, 35–36
  in subvocal linear reading, 29–
    30, 41, 89
Utah, University of, 37, 40

vision, 25–26
  peripheral, 72–73
visual reassurance, acceptance of,
  69–71, 87
visual-vertical reading, 12, 20–21,
  31, 165
  in layered reading, 71–73, 87
  reading speeds over 1,200 words
    per minute achievable
    through, 162–63, 174

visual-vertical reading (*cont'd*)
  right brain realted to, 166–67
  subvocal linear reading vs., 23
vocabulary tests, 187–88

*War and Peace* (Tolstoy), 124
Warner, Dan, 22
  class papers written by, 153–56
  mini-lessons taught by, 33–37
weekly schedules, 51–54, 66
  sample of, 53
White, E. B., 149
whole-brain experiences, 166
Wood, Evelyn:
  background of, 37–40
  brush hand motion formulated
    by, 105
  hand motions discovered by, 88
  speed reading research of, 38–39
Evelyn Wood Reading Dynamics
    Institute, 40
Evelyn Wood Reading Dynamics
    Program, 34
  background of, 35
  birth of, 40

effectiveness of, 12
essential techniques involved in,
  5
getting information about, 200
initial difficulties with, 160–61
mistaken impressions about, 67
presidential praise for, 7
study habits and performance
    transformed as result of, 159
test-taking using, 159–60
universal applicability of, 13–15
word processors, first drafts written
  on, 148–49
word:
  as keys, 135, 139, 191–93
  out of normal, expected order,
    68–69, 87
  reading in groups of, 18
writing papers, 78–79
  *see also* class papers
writing surfaces, 26

X hand motions, 97–98, 108
  diagram of, 98
  execution of, 97